Official MENSA
Puzzle Book

# *303*
# Perplexing
# Chess Puzzles

*Fred Wilson*
*&*
*Bruce Alberston*

**Sterling Publishing Co., Inc.**
New York

# ACKNOWLEDGMENTS

*We are especially grateful to Jill Meadows whose deft touch on the computer created the format, diagrams, and text, and also to Woman International Master Anca Andriana whose solving, proofreading, and analytical skills were indispensible to us. Others who contributed positions, checked solutions, or made useful suggestions are Tom Schrade, Jeremy Gross, Ross Mechanic, Mike Senkiewicz, Emmitt Jefferson, Joshua Revesz, Steve Anderson, Michele Lance, Sari Glickstein, Glen Hart, Andy Ansel, Andy Fox, Ned Wall, Nathan Resika, Jeff Tannenbaum, Ken Calitri, Jonathan Phanstiel, Anthony Daniel, Angie Cohen, Yadey Yawand-Wossen, Riley Kellogg, Rita Kelly, Marianna Loosemore, and Peter J. Tamburro, Jr. Special thanks to Glenn Petersen and Peter Gordon for their conscientious attention to the manuscript. They made it better.*

Mensa and the distinctive table logo are trademarks of American Mensa, Ltd. (in the U.S.), British Mensa, Ltd. (in the U.K.), and Mensa International Limited (in other countries) and are used by permission.

Mensa as an organization does not express an opinion as being that of Mensa or have any ideological, philosophical, political or religious affiliations. Mensa specifically disclaims any responsibility for any liability, loss or risk, personal or otherwise, which is incurred as a consequence, directly or indirectly, of the use and application of any of the contents of this book.

### Library of Congress Cataloging-in-Publication Data

Wilson, Fred.
   303 perplexing chess puzzles / Fred Wilson & Bruce Alberston.
      p. cm. — (Official Mensa puzzle book)
   Includes index.
   ISBN 1-4027-1146-8
   1. Chess problems. I. Title: Three hundred three perplexing
chess puzzles. II. Title: Three hundred and three perplexing chess
puzzles. III. Alberston, Bruce. IV. Title. V. Series.

GV1451.W72 2004
794.1'2—dc22                                   2004017598

2   4   6   8   10   9   7   5   3   1

Published by Sterling Publishing Co., Inc.
387 Park Avenue South, New York, NY 10016
© 2004 by Fred Wilson and Bruce Alberston
Distributed in Canada by Sterling Publishing
C/o Canadian Manda Group, 165 Dufferin Street
Toronto, Ontario, Canada M6K 3H6
Distributed in Great Britain by Chrysalis Books Group PLC
The Chrysalis Building, Bramley Road, London W10 6SP, England
Distributed in Australia by Capricorn Link (Australia) Pty. Ltd.
P.O. Box 704, Windsor, NSW 2756, Australia

Sterling ISBN 1-4027-1146-8

# CONTENTS

# INTRODUCTION

*The mistakes are all there, just waiting to be made.*
—Dr. Saviely Tartakower

*I missed a shot!*
—every chess player

Isaac Bashevis Singer, the Nobel Prize–winning Yiddish novelist, observed during an interview that "chess is the fairest of games since nothing is hidden from you." To which we would add, probably at the top of our lungs, only if you can *see* the tactical possibilities for both sides inherent in most positions. As we said in our last tactical workbook, *303 Tactical Chess Puzzles* (Sterling, 2002), "the only way for the advanced beginner or intermediate player to improve to the next level is to consistently study tactics." This has not changed. We still bemoan the fact, which as chess teachers we see all the time, that many talented children and adults fail to improve at chess because they have not made solving tactical chess puzzles a part of their daily routine. While most of you would not consider playing baseball, basketball, doing yoga, running, or whatever without training, it amazes us how many chess players feel it unnecessary to exercise their mental chess muscles by consistently solving tactical problems. Indeed, almost every beginner and intermediate player we know who has really improved, has worn to shreds at least one if not several works on chess tactics. So, here we are again with another tactical workbook designed to make the work you need to do to beef up your tactics not only comfortable, but enjoyable.

As in our previous tactics collections, we use only two large, clear diagrams per page to make it easier for you to concentrate. Also, we have added a hint in parentheses above each position, telling you what tactic (or tactics) you should be looking for. While we have grouped the positions in each chapter usually by order of difficulty rather than the specific tactic used, there is a

Tactics Index at the end for those who wish to study only examples of a single tactic at one time. As always, in our books, at least one-third of the positions are *"Black to move"* since we believe it is also essential to study chess diagrams from Black's perspective. As in *303 Tactical Chess Puzzles*, we continue to use a simple scoring system (devised by Bruce Alberston) to rate your current chess strength. It is described in detail in the introductions to the first three chapters. We hope you will use the scoring system the first time you work through our book, and then if you *really* want to get better, go through the book at least two more times, continuing to score yourself. We are sure your score will increase with each trip through the book along with your tactical ability in over-the-board play.

We have addressed the vast majority of the material in this book to the three largest groups of players: advanced beginner, intermediate player, and tournament player. In each of the first three chapters, the level of difficulty in the 100 chosen positions is usually reflected by the number of moves, or "ply," necessary to find in order to solve them. Literally, the word "ply" in chess means a half move or a move for one side only. In other words, a three-ply solution simply means "I do this, you do that, I do this, and now I am either winning, or have at least improved my position." Typically, most (but not all) puzzles in Chapter One are three-ply, such as the position at right.

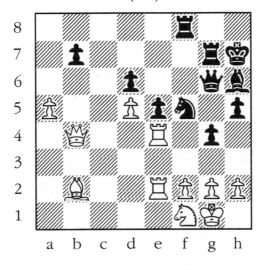

*White to move*
(Pin)

Here Gary Kasparov, the world's top-ranked player, has just moved his rook from f7 to g7 against the computer program X3D Fritz in the second game of their match on November 13, 2003, in New York City. Do you see why this was a blunder? After 1 Rxe5! dxe5 2 Qxf8 wins a pawn, and subsequently the game. Even a world champion can overlook a three-ply tactic!

Here is another slightly more complicated three-ply puzzle. Can you solve it?

**Black to move**
(Mating attack)

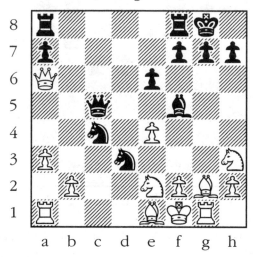

If you are having trouble with this position, it is because you are not sufficiently familiar with the tactical concept of *smothered mate*. The answer is 1 ... Qxf2+!, with two variations: 2 Bxf2 Nd2# or 2 Nxf2 Ne3#. All of the White king's escape squares are occupied by his own pieces!

In Chapter Two, most of the solutions are five-ply in length (but not all—we have thrown in a couple of longer ones to keep you on your toes!) and require you to visualize a slightly longer sequence. Here is an interesting position with White to move, where if Black is allowed one consolidating move (such as 1 ... Ne6), he can probably survive. How can White strike quickly and decisively?

*White to move*
(Deflection/mating attack)

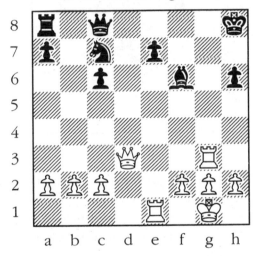

Did you notice that Black's bishop is *overloaded*, that it must guard both e7 and the a1/h1 diagonal? If you did, then you found 1 Rxe7 Bxe7 2 Qd4+ Kg8 (or h7) 3 Qg7#. If Black does not capture the rook, there follows a quick mate at h7.

Again, another five-ply position, which you should solve quickly.

**White to move**
(Double attack)

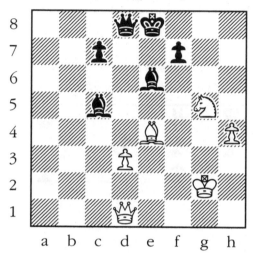

Did you look at all your *forcing moves* (i.e., checks and captures)? If so, then you found 1 Nxe6 fxe6 2 Qh5+ Kd7 3 Qxc5 winning a piece. Even after 3 ... Qxh4 4 Bc6+ Kc8 5 Qf8+ Qd8 6 Qxd8+ Kxd8, White has an easy win as long as he prevents the exchange of his last pawn.

In Chapter Three, basically aimed at the so-called tournament or advanced players, almost all of the solutions are seven-ply in length or longer, and, of course, we've perversely added a few that are only five-ply in length, but rather difficult. At right is a seemingly equal position in which White has just moved his knight to c4. Can you discover why this was a blunder?

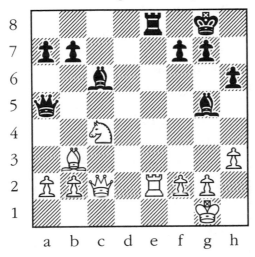

We actually gave you quite a clue when mentioning *x-ray*. So, of course you saw that Black is actually attacking e1 twice, and thus, 1 … Qe1+! 2 Rxe1 Rxe1+ 3 Kh2 Bf4+ 4 g3 Rh1#.

Now don't be scared because the following position is actually at least eleven-ply; it is a pretty straightforward calculation if you can get the right idea. In the endgame below from B. Zuckerman – A. Mengarini, Philadelphia, 1971, in response to Black's move … c5+!, White quite mistakenly played his king to e4 in a fruitless winning attempt, when he could have drawn easily by going to c3 or d3. How was he punished?

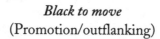

*Black to move*
(Promotion/outflanking)

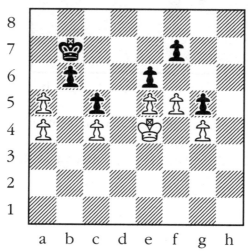

1 … Ka6!! 2 axb6 Kxb6 3 Kd3 Ka5 4 Kc2 Kxa4 5 Kc3 Ka3 6 Kc2 Kb4 and White resigned. The king and pawn ending is hopeless.

Additionally, it occurs to us that you may wonder if it is possible to create two or even one-ply puzzles which can be taxing. Believe it or not, the devilish puzzle on the next page, created by Bruce Alberston for our *202 Surprising Checkmates* (1998), is only one-ply!

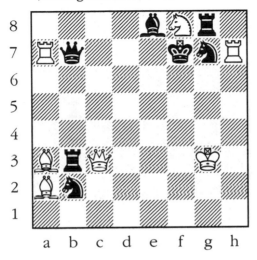

Now, mates in two or three moves are not acceptable. Find a mate in one! Answer: 1 Qf3#! Yes, a pinned piece can give mate!

Finally, an amusing, two-ply problem which GM V. Tukmakov recently failed to solve in his game against GM L. Kritz at the Biel Masters Tournament, 2003.

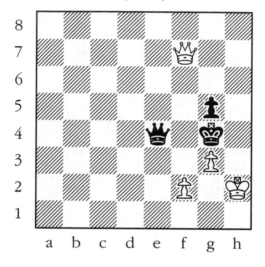

GM Tukmakov, probably in time pressure, missed 1 ... Qg2+ 2 Kxg2 *stalemate*, and eventually even lost.

Recently, on his internet radio chess show, *Chess & Books With Fred Wilson*, broadcast from the website www.Chess.FM, Fred interviewed Grandmasters Larry Christiansen and Joel Benjamin on consecutive weeks. He asked each of them the same question: "Did you ever have to specifically study tactics as a child or were you always able to visualize three to five-ply when playing?" Both replied that they could not remember ever going out of their way to study tactics in general, let alone set up a consistent routine for solving combinations. Mostly, they both studied openings and played over complete games. Well, while this obviously works for that tiny group of people with enormous chess talent, *the rest of us mere mortals have got to put a great deal of effort into studying chess tactics or we will never achieve our highest possible level of chess skill.* It's as simple as that.

Get started!

—Fred Wilson & Bruce Alberston

# CHAPTER ONE
## 100 POSITIONS FOR THE ADVANCED BEGINNER

**The Advanced Beginner:** Just who is the advanced beginner? Well, he (or she) happens to be your average chess player. He's thoroughly conversant with the moves and rules, and he's had some limited exposure to the basic concepts of the opening, middlegame, and ending. What he lacks is the experience to put everything together into a coherent whole. What he also lacks is the tactical ability to lift his game to a higher plane. Hopefully, our book will help remedy this particular deficiency.

Anyway, the problems in this chapter are geared to the level of our hypothetical average advanced beginner. He's expected to solve the majority of the positions (over 50%), but we also expect him to do some stretching. The stretching is important if you want to move up a class in strength.

**Scoring:** Scoring is optional, but if you want to keep track, here's how to do it. There are a hundred positions in the chapter, each one worth one point. Give yourself full credit if you worked out the main line of the solution. And if you found only the first move, you can still give yourself a half-point part credit. As for the two bonus positions at the end of the chapter, don't worry if you miss them, but take credit if you solve them and add on to your score.

We would also like to see intermediate and tournament players trying their hand at this chapter. The chart below shows the average expected score for each category of player.

| Player Category | Average number of positions correctly solved, out of 100 | Average number of positions incorrectly solved, out of 100 |
|---|---|---|
| Advanced Beginner | 64 | 36 |
| Intermediate Player | 76 | 24 |
| Tournament Player | 92 | 8 |

## 1.
### *White to move*
### (Mating attack)

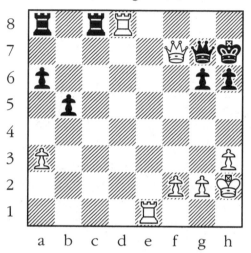

## 2.
### *White to move*
### (Trapping)

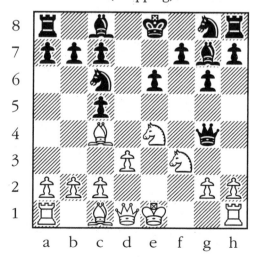

## 3.

*White to move*
(Driving off)

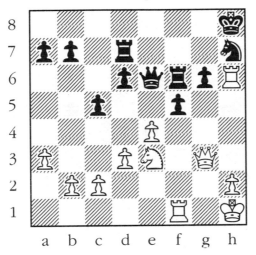

## 4.

*Black to move*
(Pin)

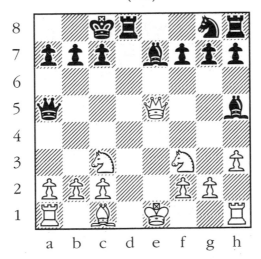

## 5.
*White to move*
(Mating attack)

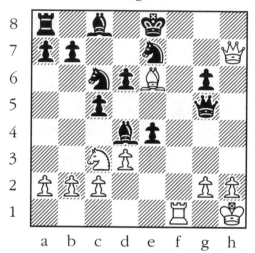

## 6.
*White to move*
(Removing the guard)

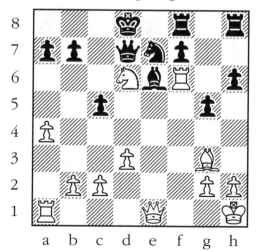

# 7.

### *White to move*
### (Zwischenschach)

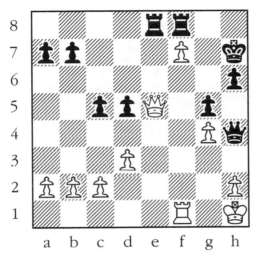

# 8.

### *White to move*
### (Overload)

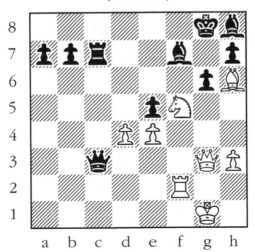

**9.**
*White to move*
(Clearance/mating attack)

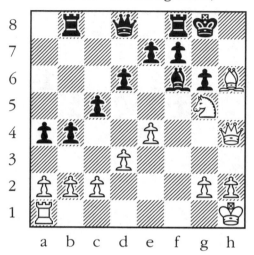

**10.**
*White to move*
(Trapping)

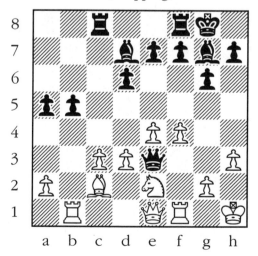

## 11.
### *Black to move*
(Pin)

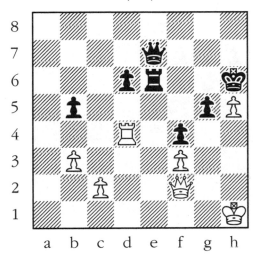

## 12.
### *Black to move*
(Pin/mating attack)

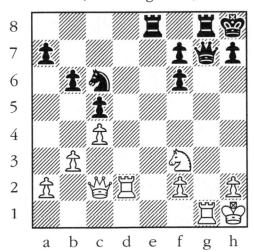

## 13.
### *White to move*
(Removing the guard)

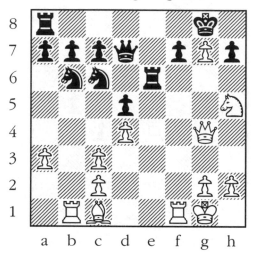

## 14.
### *White to move*
(Discovery/mating attack)

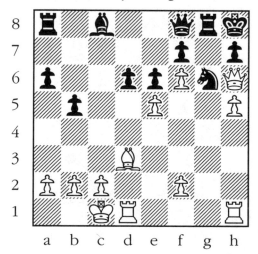

**15.**
*White to move*
(Double check)

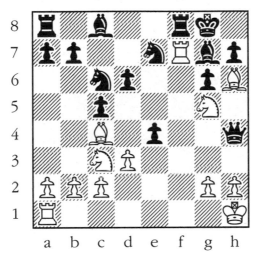

**16.**
*White to move*
(Pin)

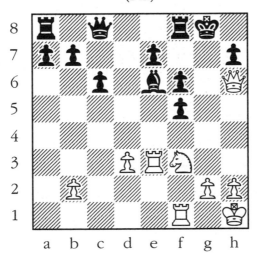

## 17.
*White to move*
(Deflection/mating attack)

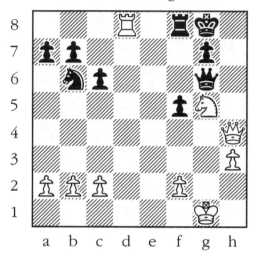

## 18.
*White to move*
(Driving off)

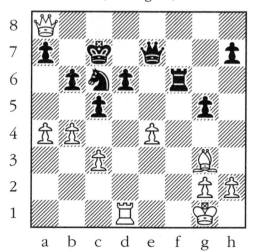

## 19.
### *White to move*
(Discovery)

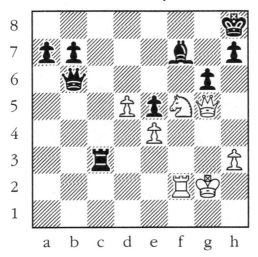

## 20.
### *White to move*
(Mating attack)

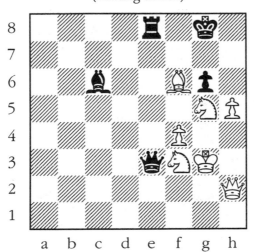

## 21.
### *White to move*
(Double threat)

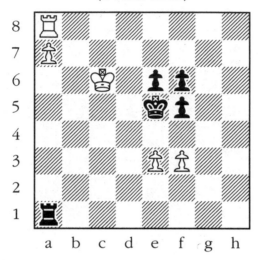

## 22.
### *White to move*
(Promotion)

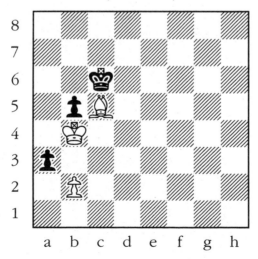

## 23.
### *White to move*
(Pin)

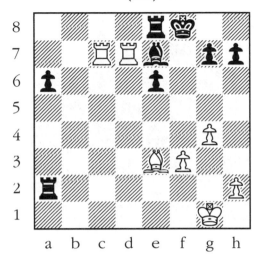

## 24.
### *Black to move*
(Deflection)

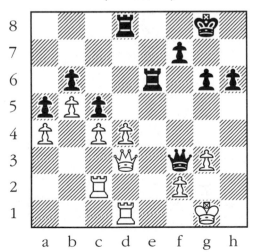

## 25.
### White to move
### (Mating attack)

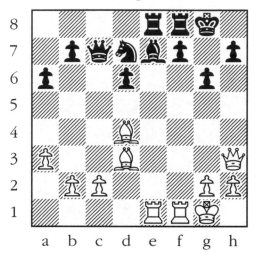

## 26.
### White to move
### (Pin)

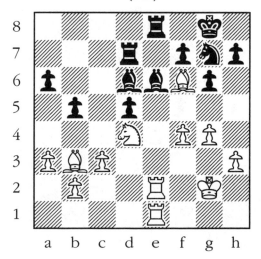

**27.**

*White to move*

(En prise)

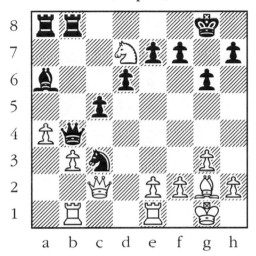

**28.**

*Black to move*

(Trapping)

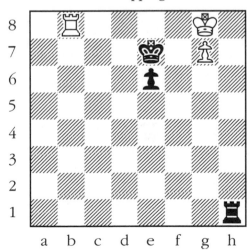

## 29.
*Black to move*
(Pin)

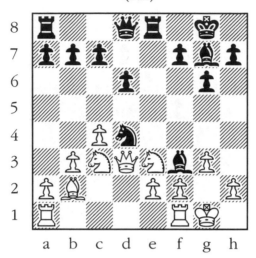

## 30.
*White to move*
(Pin)

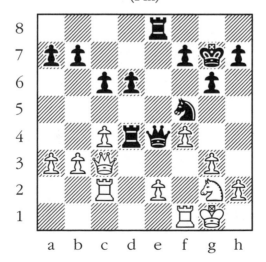

**31.**

*White to move*

(Removing the guard)

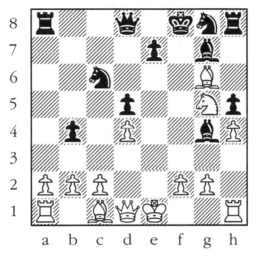

**32.**

*White to move*

(Mating attack)

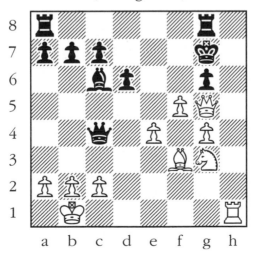

## 33.

*White to move*

(Removing the guard/mating attack)

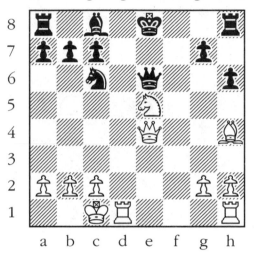

## 34.

*White to move*

(Fork)

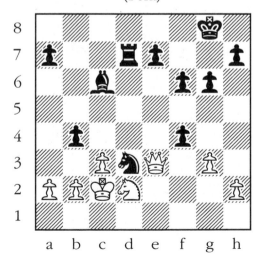

## 35.
### *Black to move*
### (Pin)

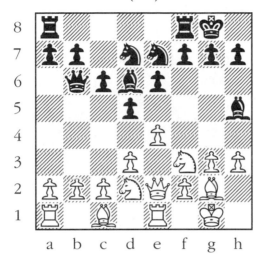

## 36.
### *Black to move*
### (Overload)

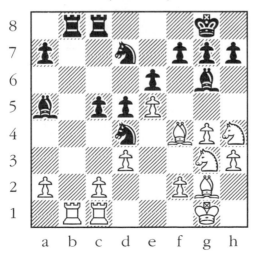

## 37.
*White to move*
(Double threat)

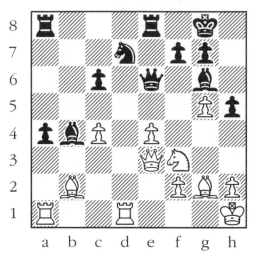

## 38.
*White to move*
(Discovery)

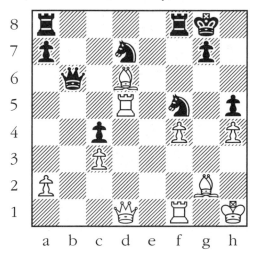

## 39.
### *White to move*
(Interference)

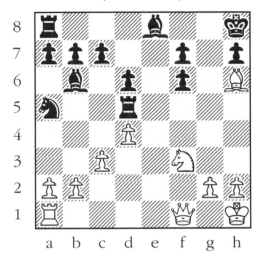

## 40.
### *White to move*
(Pin)

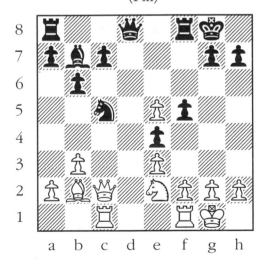

## 41.
### *White to move*
(Discovery)

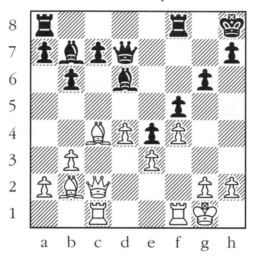

## 42.
### *White to move*
(Deflection/mating attack)

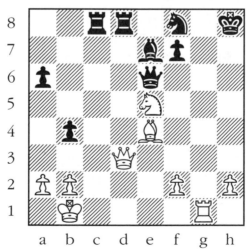

## 43.
### *White to move*
(Deflection/mating attack)

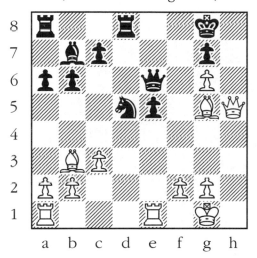

## 44.
### *Black to move*
(Pin)

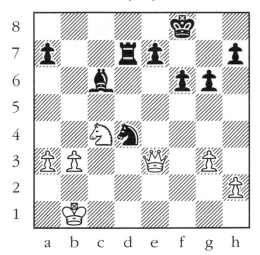

## 45.
### *White to move*
(Discovery)

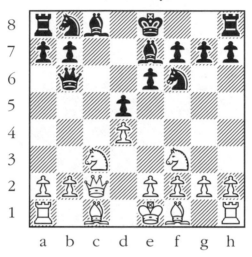

## 46.
### *Black to move*
(Unpin)

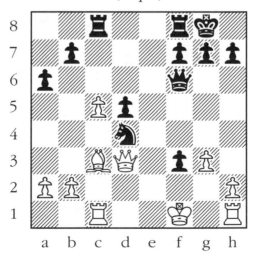

## 47.
### *White to move*
(Mating attack)

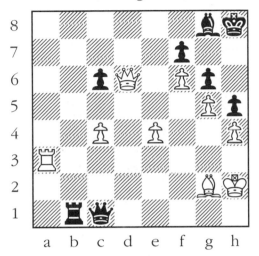

## 48.
### *White to move*
(Fork)

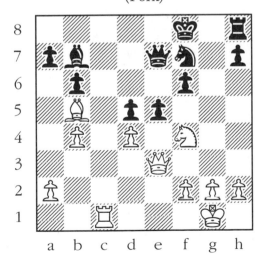

## 49.
### *Black to move*
#### (Mating attack)

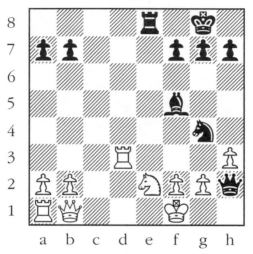

## 50.
### *White to move*
#### (Discovery)

## 51.
### *White to move*
(Mating attack)

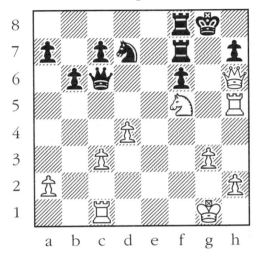

## 52.
### *Black to move*
(Simplification)

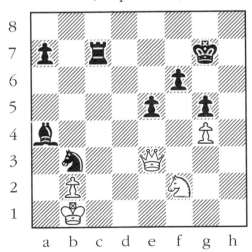

## 53.
*White to move*
(Promotion)

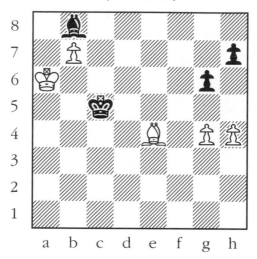

## 54.
*White to move*
(Removing the guard)

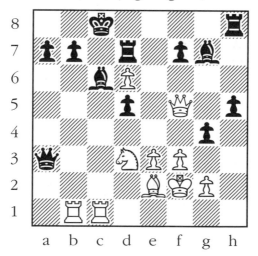

## 55.
### White to move
### (Fork)

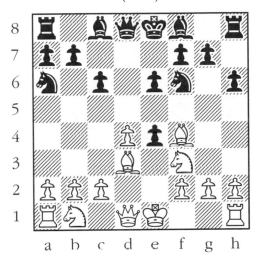

## 56.
### Black to move
### (En prise)

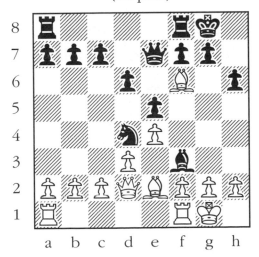

## 57.
### *Black to move*
(Mating attack)

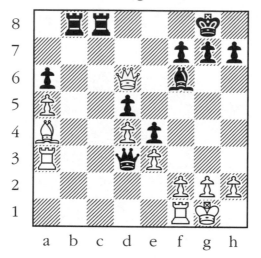

## 58.
### *Black to move*
(Removing the guard)

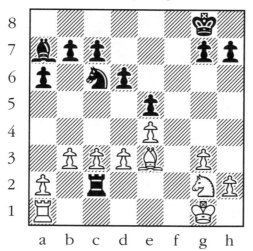

## 59.
### *Black to move*
(En prise)

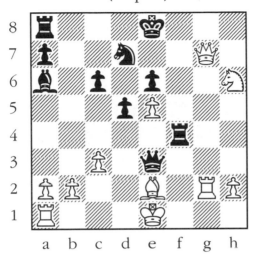

## 60.
### *White to move*
(Skewer)

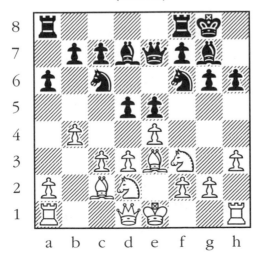

## 61.
### *Black to move*
(Removing the guard)

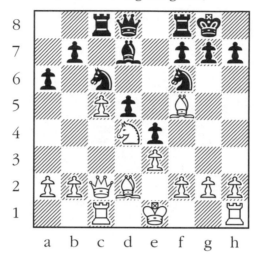

## 62.
### *Black to move*
(Fork)

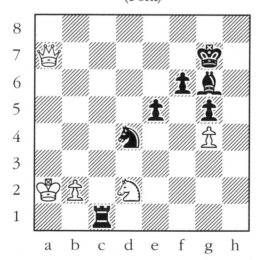

## 63.
### *White to move*
(Deflection/Mating attack)

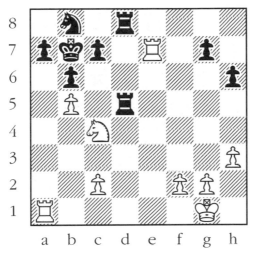

## 64.
### *Black to move*
(Fork)

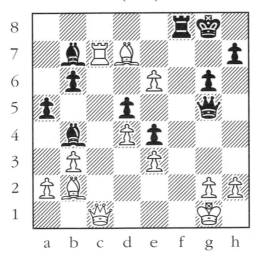

## 65.
### Black to move
(Discovery)

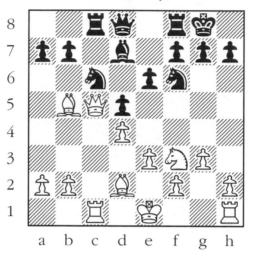

## 66.
### Black to move
(En prise)

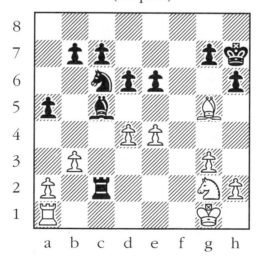

## 67.
### Black to move
### (Pin)

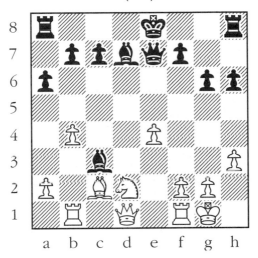

## 68.
### White to move
### (Mating attack)

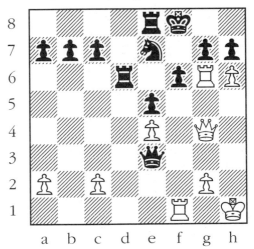

## 69.
### Black to move
(Mating attack)

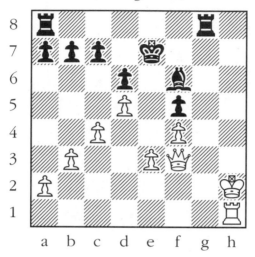

## 70.
### White to move
(Removing the guard)

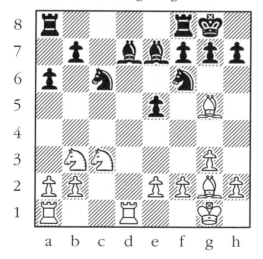

## 71.
### *Black to move*
(Fork)

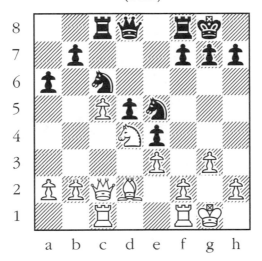

## 72.
### *White to move*
(Removing the guard)

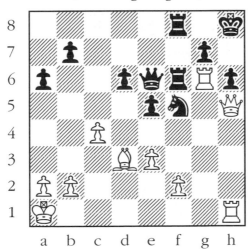

**73.**

*White to move*

(Removing the guard)

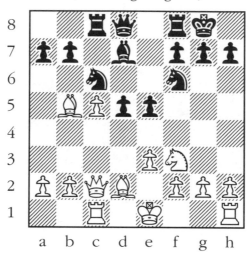

**74.**

*Black to move*

(Discovery)

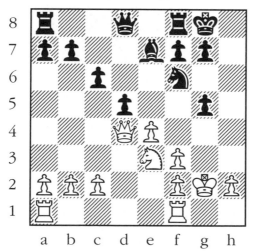

## 75.
*Black to move*
(Pin)

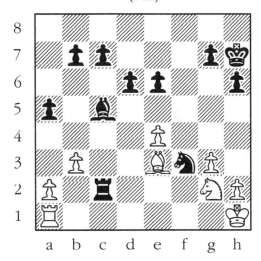

## 76.
*Black to move*
(Unpin)

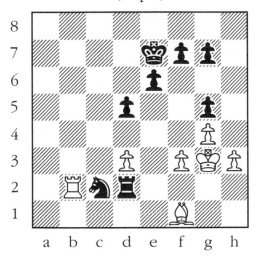

## 77.
*White to move*
(Overload)

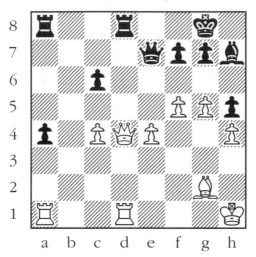

## 78.
*Black to move*
(Removing the guard)

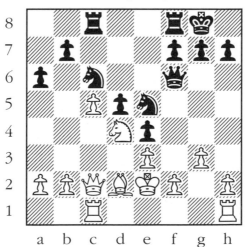

## 79.
### Black to move
### (Pin)

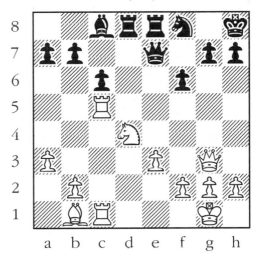

## 80.
### Black to move
### (En prise)

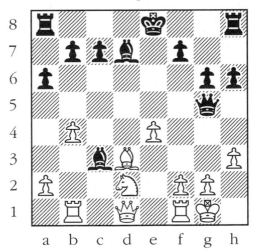

## 81.
### *White to move*
(Deflection)

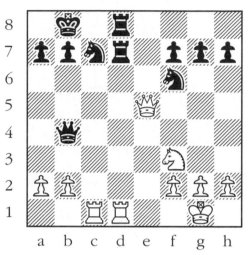

## 82.
### *White to move*
(Pin)

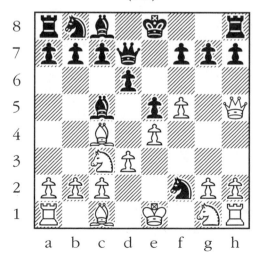

## 83.
### Black to move
### (Skewer)

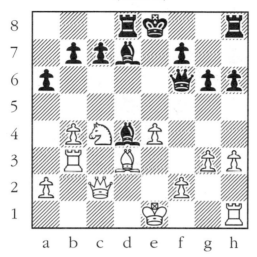

## 84.
### Black to move
### (Zwischenschach)

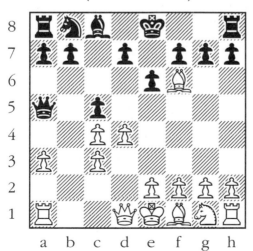

## 85.
### Black to move
### (Discovery)

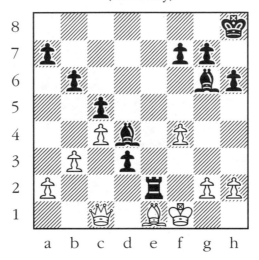

## 86.
### Black to move
### (Driving off)

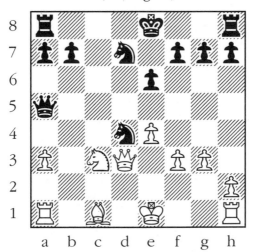

## 87.
*Black to move*
(X-ray)

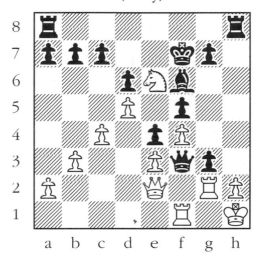

## 88.
*Black to move*
(Fork)

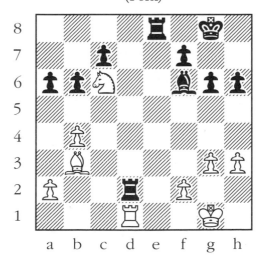

## 89.
### *White to move*
(Removing the guard)

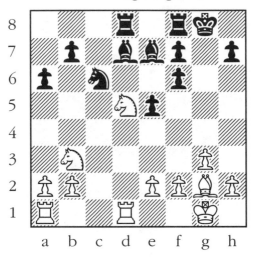

## 90.
### *White to move*
(En prise)

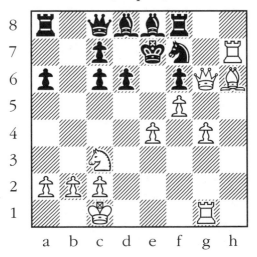

## 91.
### *Black to move*
(Promotion)

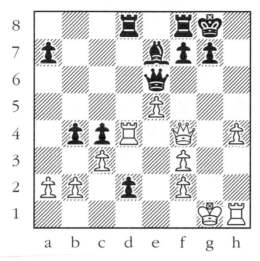

## 92.
### *White to move*
(Driving off/double attack)

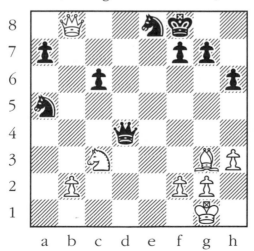

## 93.
### Black to move
(En prise)

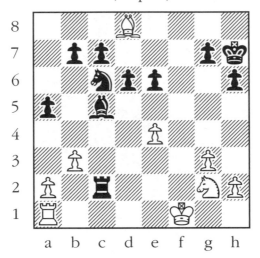

## 94.
### Black to move
(En prise)

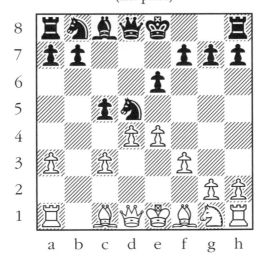

## 95.
### *White to move*
(Discovery/fork)

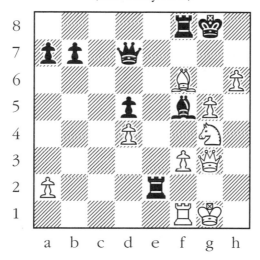

## 96.
### *White to move*
(Trapping)

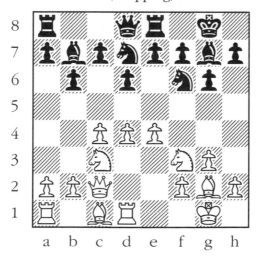

## 97.
### *Black to move*
(Fork)

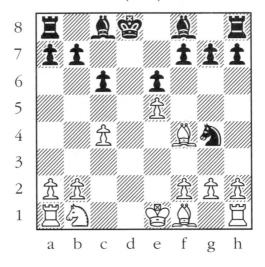

## 98.
### *Black to move*
(Removing the guard)

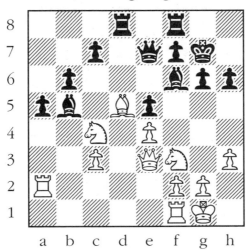

## 99.
### Black to move
(En prise)

## 100.
### White to move
(Mating attack)

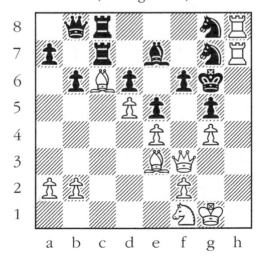

## 100A.
### *White to move*
(Fork)

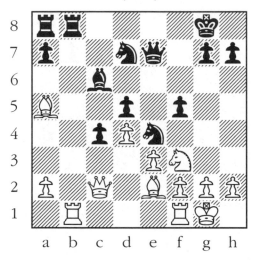

## 100B.
### *White to move*
(Trapping)

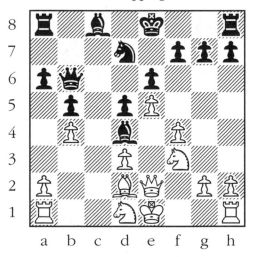

# CHAPTER TWO
# 100 POSITIONS FOR THE INTERMEDIATE PLAYER

**The Intermediate Player:** The intermediate player is a cut above the national average. He's advanced to the level where he can now crush the random player on the block. He's read several chess books and he's been exposed to some of the more advanced concepts of the game. If he has a computer, he's likely played some games on the Internet. Also probable is that he's competed in a couple of tournaments, but is not yet a full-fledged tournament player.

Intermediate is a decent player who doesn't often beat himself. Nevertheless, something is lacking in the play. And what seems to be missing is consistency throughout the course of the entire game. Sometimes it's there, sometimes it's not. When it's not, the culprit is usually some tactical trick that's escaped his line of sight. It is one of those ornery gaps in tactical technique that has yet to become second nature. When it gets down to the fingertips, and you don't have to think about it, that's when consistency improves.

**Scoring:** Keeping score of your results is not required. But if you want to maintain a record, there is a way we suggest you go about it. Award yourself one full point for a problem correctly solved, right through to the end of the main line. If you got just the first two moves of the solution, take a half-point part credit. The two bonus positions at the end of the chapter cannot hurt your score if you miss them. But they can improve your score if you get them right. That's what a bonus is for.

The positions in this chapter are laid out largely for the intermediate level player. But we hope they will also be used by the advanced beginner and the tournament-level player. The average expected score by each class of player is shown in the chart below.

| Player Category | Average number of positions correctly solved, out of 100 | Average number of positions incorrectly solved, out of 100 |
|---|---|---|
| Advanced Beginner | 36 | 64 |
| Intermediate Player | 64 | 36 |
| Tournament Player | 85 | 15 |

## 101.
### *Black to move*
(Discovery/mating attack)

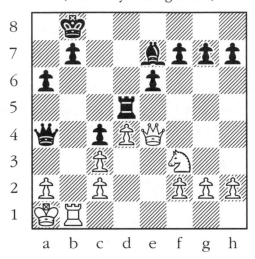

## 102.
### *White to move*
(Driving off)

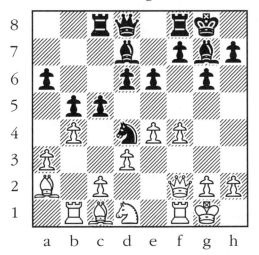

## 103.
### *White to move*
(Pin)

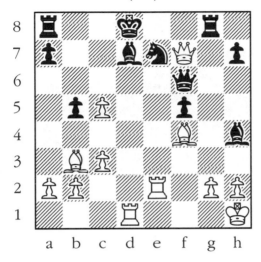

## 104.
### *White to move*
(Skewer/Fork)

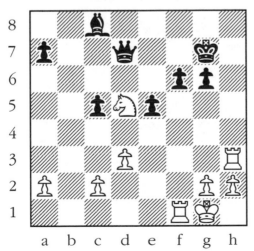

## 105.
*White to move*
(Removing the guard/discovery)

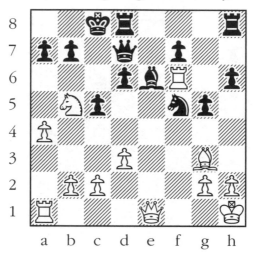

## 106.
*White to move*
(Trapping)

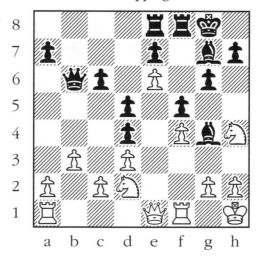

## 107.
### *Black to move*
(Removing the Guard)

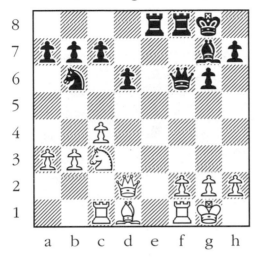

## 108.
### *White to move*
(Line opening/closing)

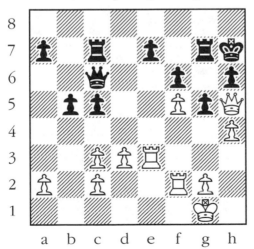

## 109.
### *White to move*
(Deflection)

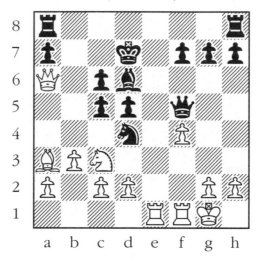

## 110.
### *White to move*
(Mating attack)

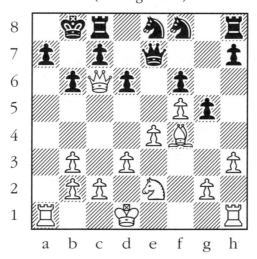

## 111.

*White to move*
(Mating attack)

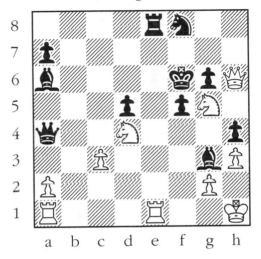

## 112.

*White to move*
(Discovery)

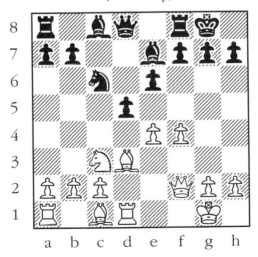

## 113.
### *White to move*
(Pin)

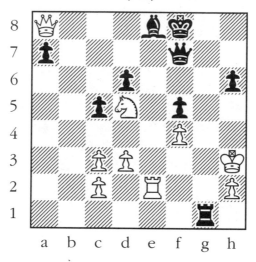

## 114.
### *White to move*
(Mating attack)

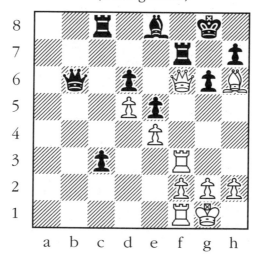

## 115.
### *White to move*
(Mating attack)

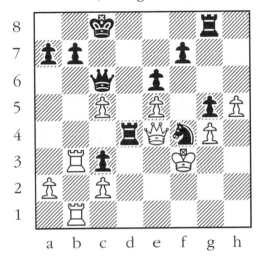

## 116.
### *Black to move*
(Attraction/mating attack)

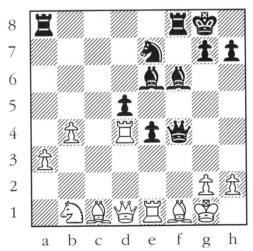

## 117.
### *Black to move*
(Deflection)

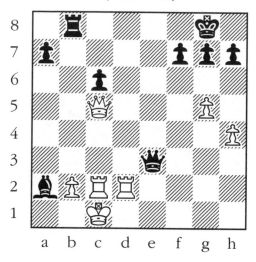

## 118.
### *White to move*
(Driving off)

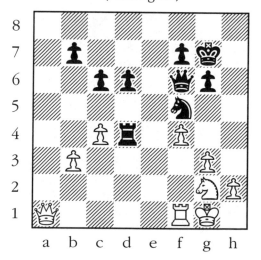

## 119.
### *White to move*
(Fork)

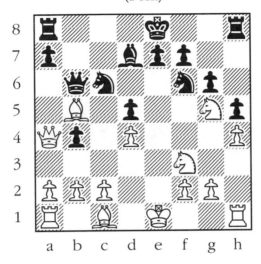

## 120.
### *Black to move*
(Skewer)

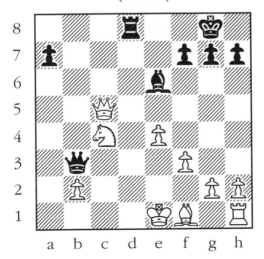

## 121.
### *Black to move*
(Pin)

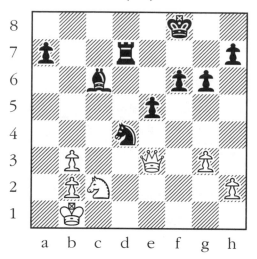

## 122.
### *White to move*
(Promotion)

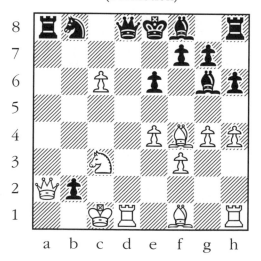

## 123.
### *White to move*
(Fork)

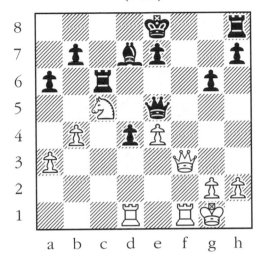

## 124.
### *White to move*
(Mating attack)

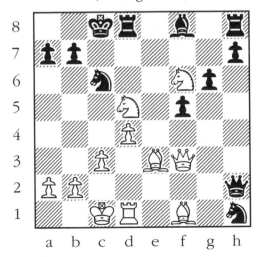

## 125.
*White to move*
(Removing the guard/fork)

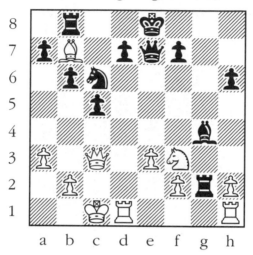

## 126.
*Black to move*
(Removing the guard)

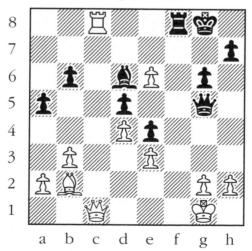

## 127.

*Black to move*
(Deflection/mating attack)

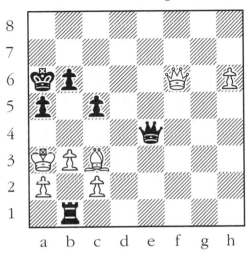

## 128.

*Black to move*
(Discovery)

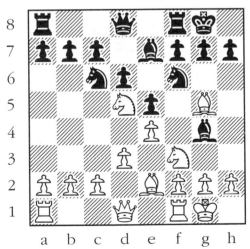

## 129.
### *Black to move*
(Mating attack)

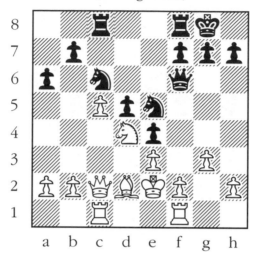

## 130.
### *Black to move*
(Pin)

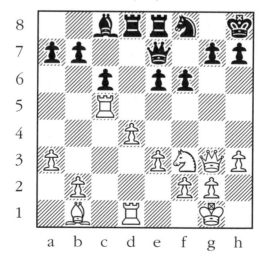

## 131.
### *White to move*
(Mating attack)

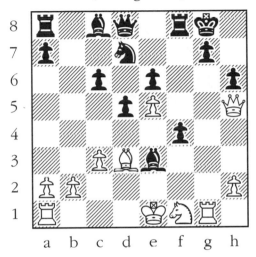

## 132.
### *Black to move*
(Removing the guard)

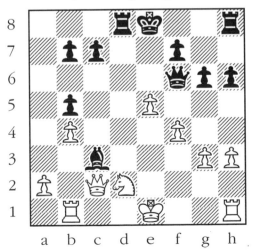

## 133.
### *White to move*
(Overload)

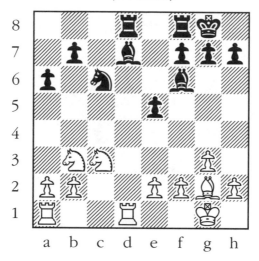

## 134.
### *White to move*
(Mating attack)

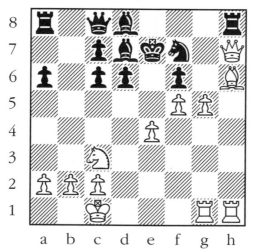

## 135.
### *White to move*
(Removing the guard)

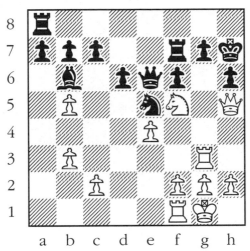

## 136.
### *White to move*
(Discovery)

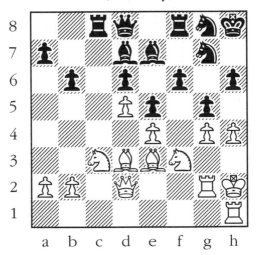

## 137.
### *Black to move*
(Mating attack)

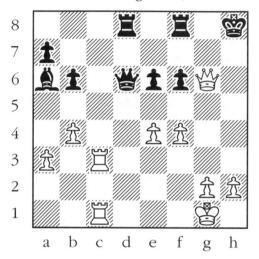

## 138.
### *White to move*
(Mating attack)

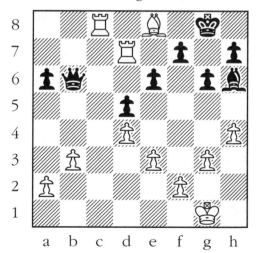

### 139.
*White to move*
(Mating attack)

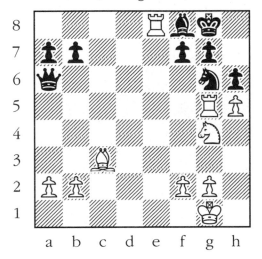

### 140.
*Black to move*
(Fork)

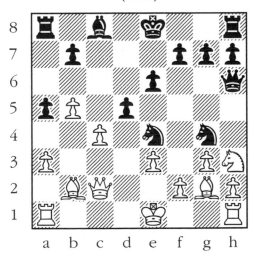

## 141.
### *White to move*
(Discovery)

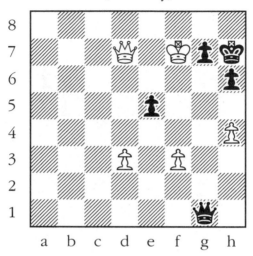

## 142.
### *White to move*
(Double threat)

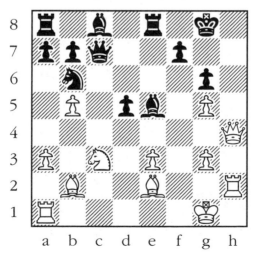

## 143.
### White to move
(Deflection)

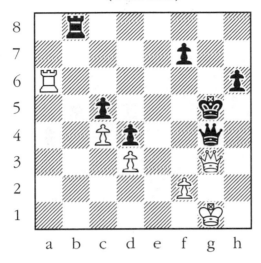

## 144.
### Black to move
(Trapping)

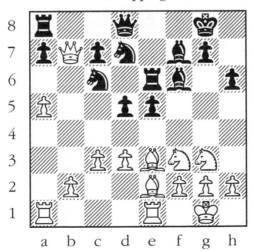

## 145.
### *White to move*
(Removing the guard)

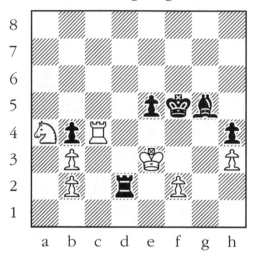

## 146.
### *Black to move*
(Removing the guard)

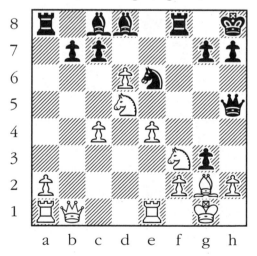

## 147.
*White to move*
(Fork)

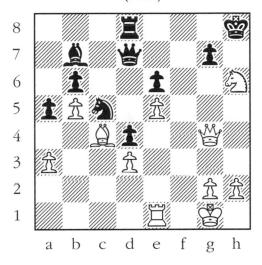

## 148.
*Black to move*
(Back rank)

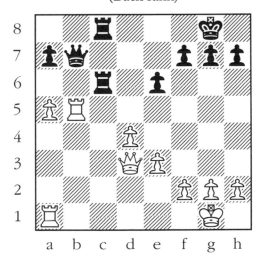

## 149.
*White to move*
(Mating attack)

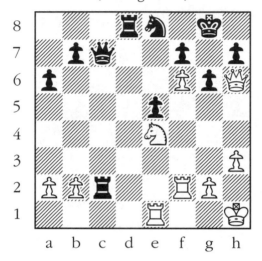

## 150.
*Black to move*
(Mating attack)

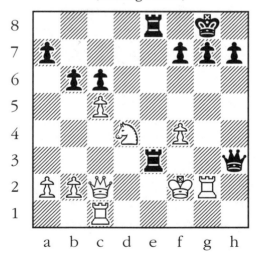

## 151.

### *Black to move*
(Removing the guard)

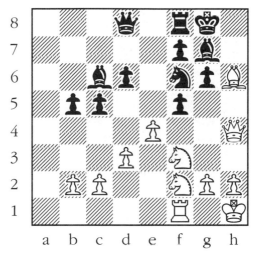

## 152.

### *Black to move*
(Removing the guard/mating attack)

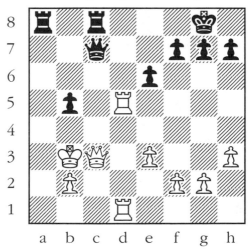

## 153.
### *White to move*
(Overload)

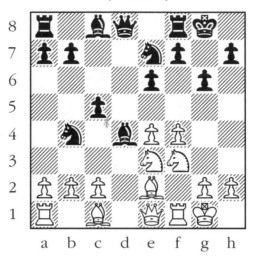

## 154.
### *White to move*
(Mating attack)

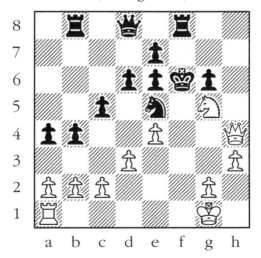

## 155.
### *White to move*
(Trapping)

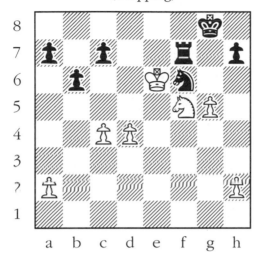

## 156.
### *White to move*
(Pin/mating attack)

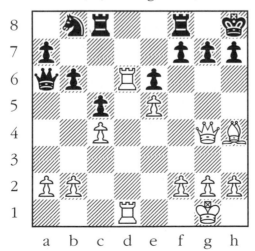

## 157.
*White to move*
(Trapping)

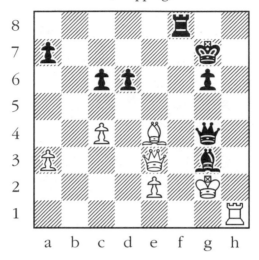

## 158.
*White to move*
(Fork)

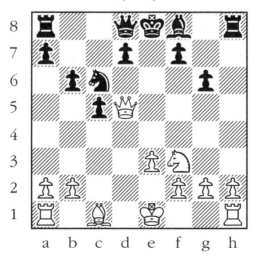

## 159.
*Black to move*
(Unpin)

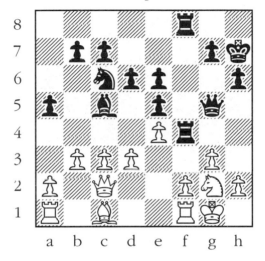

## 160.
*White to move*
(Overload)

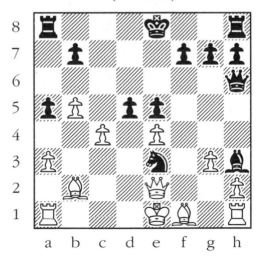

## 161.
### *White to move*
(Mating attack)

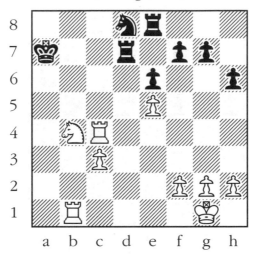

## 162.
### *White to move*
(Draw)

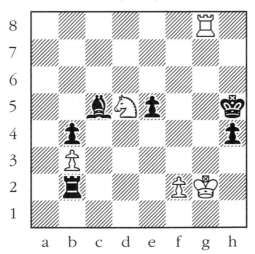

## 163.
### Black to move
(Double threat)

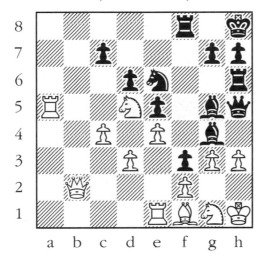

## 164.
### White to move
(Mating attack)

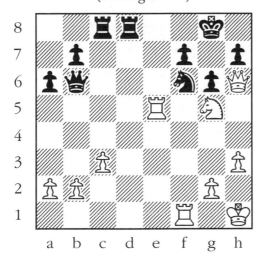

## 165.
### *White to move*
(Driving off)

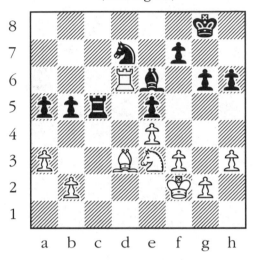

## 166.
### *White to move*
(Fork)

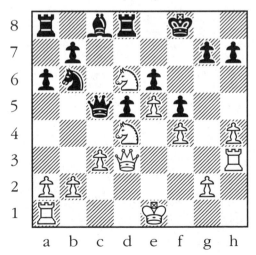

## 167.
### Black to move
(Driving off)

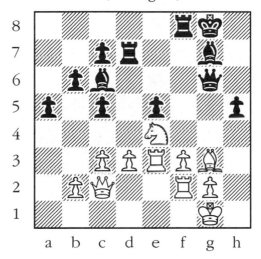

## 168.
### Black to move
(En prise)

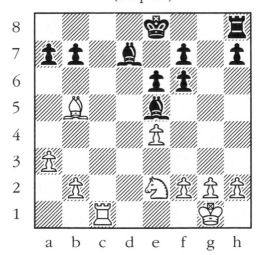

## 169.
### *White to move*
(Fork)

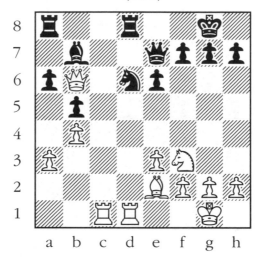

## 170.
### *Black to move*
(Trapping)

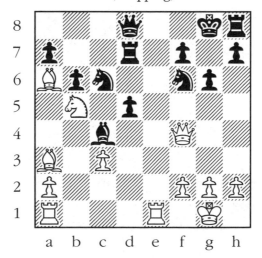

## 171.
### *White to move*
(Fork)

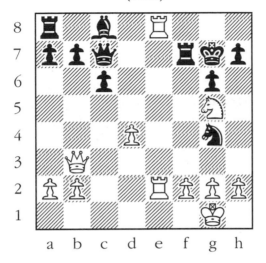

## 172.
### *White to move*
(Pin)

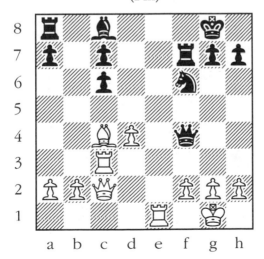

## 173.
### Black to move
(Pin)

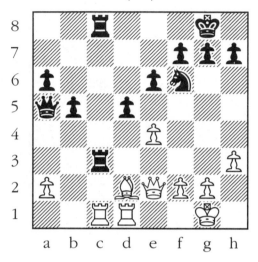

## 174.
### White to move
(Deflection)

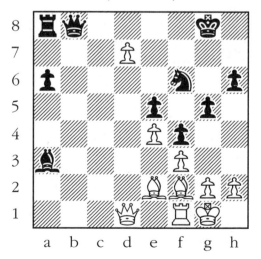

## 175.

### *White to move*
### (Mating attack)

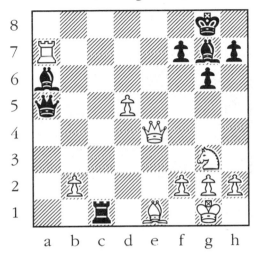

## 176.

### *White to move*
### (Mating attack)

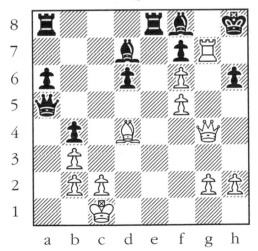

## 177.
### *White to move*
(Driving off)

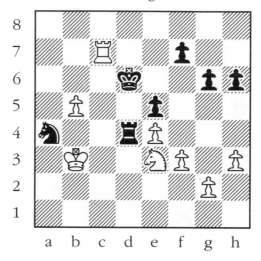

## 178.
### *White to move*
(Trapping)

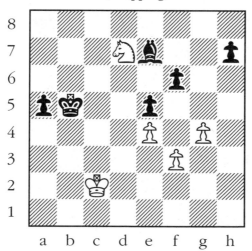

## 179.
### *White to move*
(Mating attack)

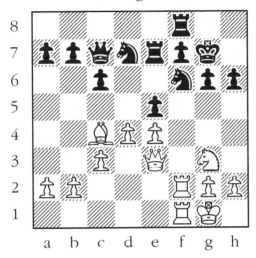

## 180.
### *White to move*
(Fork)

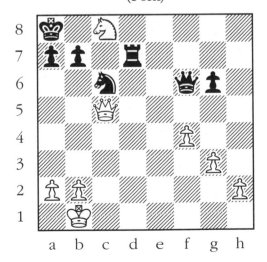

## 181.
### *Black to move*
(En prise)

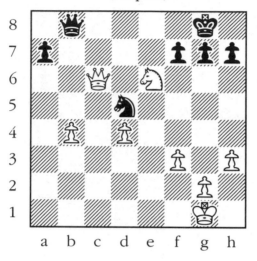

## 182.
### *Black to move*
(Mating attack)

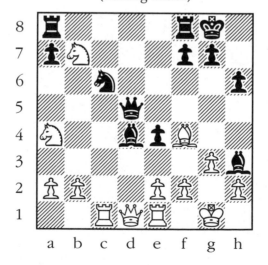

## 183.
### *White to move*
(Fork)

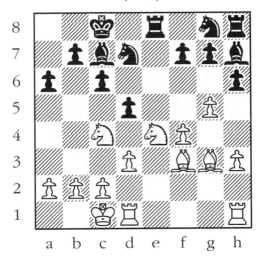

## 184.
### *Black to move*
(Driving off)

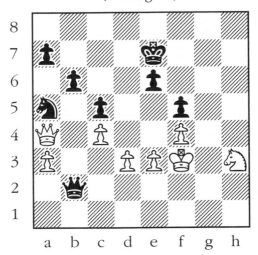

## 185.
### Black to move
(En prise)

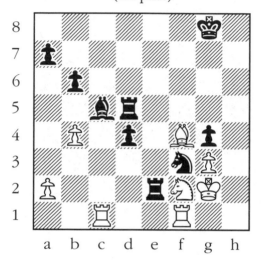

## 186.
### White to move
(Driving off)

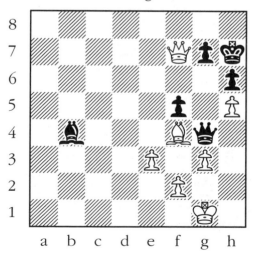

## 187.
### *White to move*
(Mating attack)

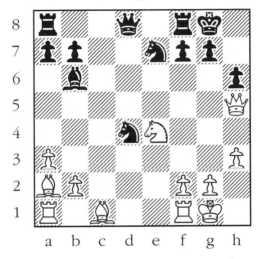

## 188.
### *Black to move*
(Trapping)

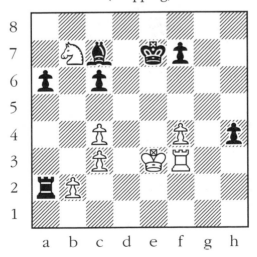

## 189.
### *Black to move*
(Mating attack)

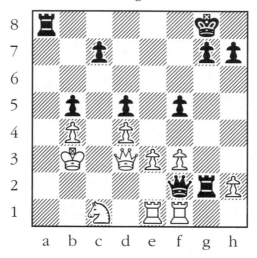

## 190.
### *Black to move*
(Mating attack)

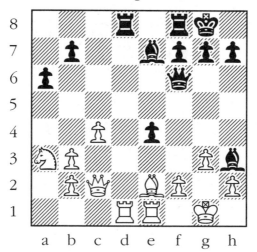

## 191.
### *White to move*
(Fork)

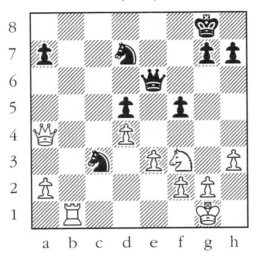

## 192.
### *White to move*
(Promotion)

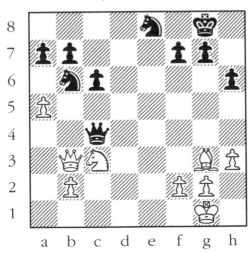

## 193.
### *White to move*
(Fork)

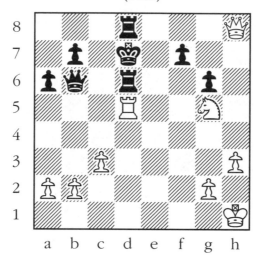

## 194.
### *White to move*
(Fork)

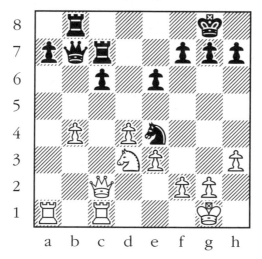

## 195.
*White to move*
(Mating attack)

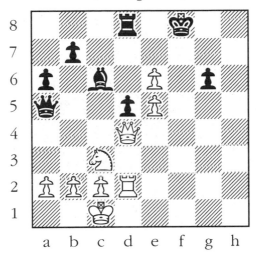

## 196.
*Black to move*
(Fork)

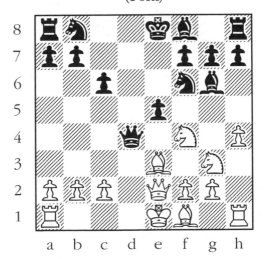

## 197.
### *Black to move*
(Removing the guard)

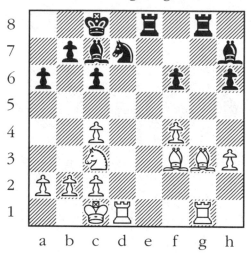

## 198.
### *White to move*
(Fork)

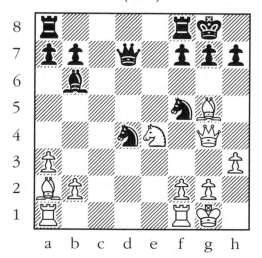

## 199.
### *White to move*
(Mating attack)

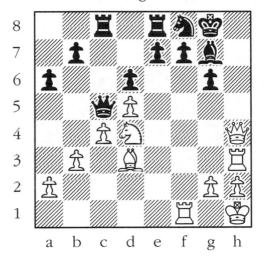

## 200.
### *White to move*
(Pin)

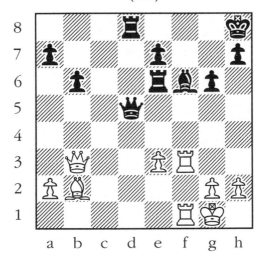

## 200A.
### *White to move*
(Mating attack)

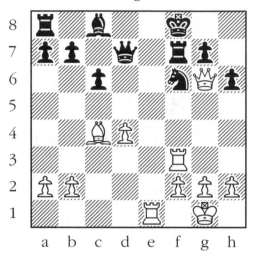

## 200B.
### *Black to move*
(Simplification)

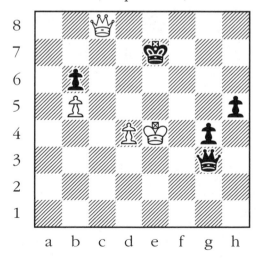

# CHAPTER THREE
# 100 POSITIONS FOR THE TOURNAMENT PLAYER

**The Tournament Player:** When we come to the tournament player we move into the arena of competitive chess. We're no longer referring to the casual amateur who uses chess as a form of recreation. Our tournament competitor is a different breed altogether. He's the serious chess player who is out to test himself and is looking to improve even more. Acquiring knowledge and experience through reading books, taking private lessons, and engaging in practical play, our tournament player has achieved a level of chess culture and technique that enables him to compete in over-the-board play with others of his own kind.

If he has talent and ability above the ordinary, then he also has aspirations of moving up to expert or master class. And if that happens, it will be accompanied by a commensurate increase in tactical acumen. That's how you get there, and this chapter will help.

**Scoring:** If you intend to measure your results, take one point full credit for each correct solution. If you can't work out the main line in its entirety, you can still take a half-point part credit for getting the first three moves of the solution. As with the previous two chapters, there are two bonus positions at the end of this one. Anyone who works through all these positions is entitled to a bonus.

Intermediate players are encouraged to try their hand at Chapter Three, but we have some reservations with respect to the beginners. Even an advanced beginner is likely to find his results disappointing. However, anyone willing to try this chapter is free to do so. We're certainly not going to stop you. The chart below indicates the average expected score for each level of player.

| Player Category | Average number of positions correctly solved, out of 100 | Average number of positions incorrectly solved, out of 100 |
|---|---|---|
| Advanced Beginner | 15 | 85 |
| Intermediate Player | 36 | 64 |
| Tournament Player | 64 | 36 |

## 201.
### *White to move*
(Mating attack)

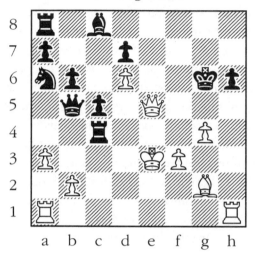

## 202.
### *White to move*
(Pin)

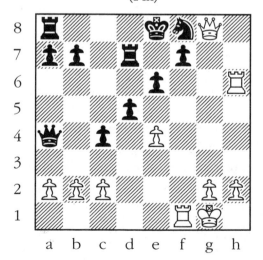

## 203.
### Black to move
(Promotion/fork)

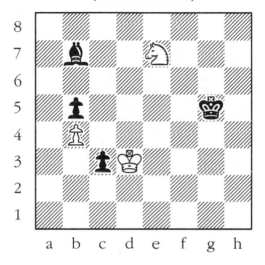

## 204.
### White to move
(Promotion)

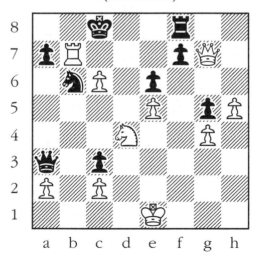

## 205.
### Black to move
(Pin)

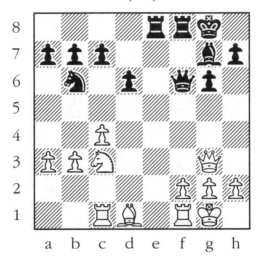

## 206.
### Black to move
(Promotion)

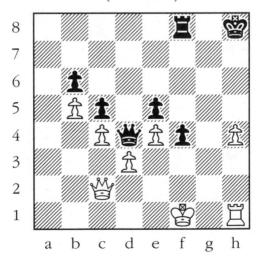

## 207.
### *White to move*
(Mating attack)

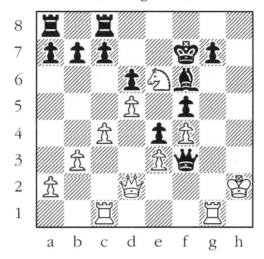

## 208.
### *Black to move*
(Mating attack)

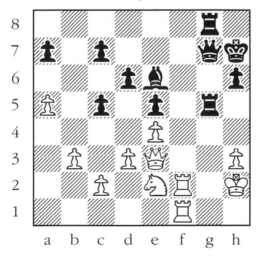

## 209.
### *White to move*
(Removing the guard)

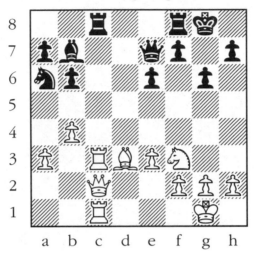

## 210.
### *White to move*
(Driving off)

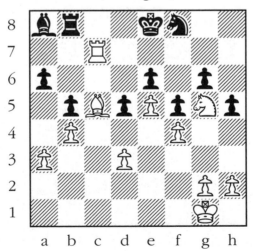

## 211.
*White to move*
(Mating attack)

## 212.
*White to move*
(Fork)

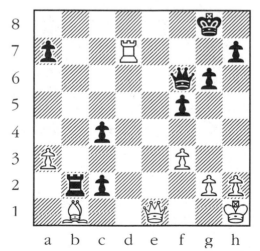

## 213.
*White to move*
(Pin)

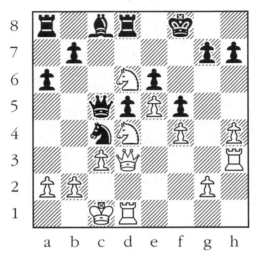

## 214.
*Black to move*
(En prise)

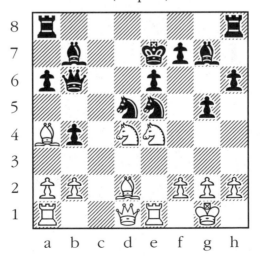

## 215.
### *White to move*
(Zugswang)

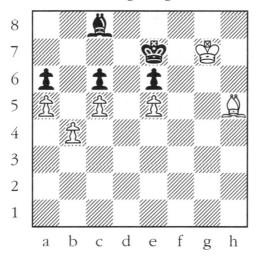

## 216.
### *White to move*
(En prise)

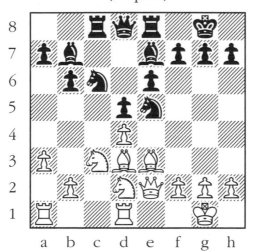

## 217.
### *Black to move*
(Fork)

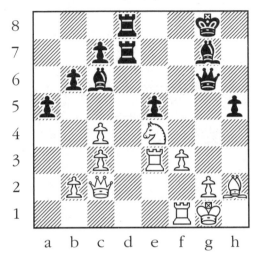

## 218.
### *White to move*
(Overload)

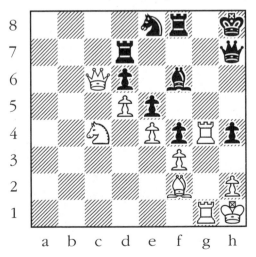

## 219.
### White to move
(Removing the guard)

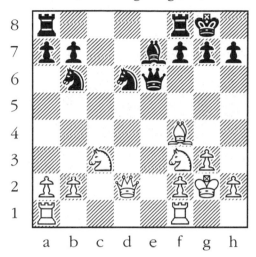

## 220.
### White to move
(Removing the guard)

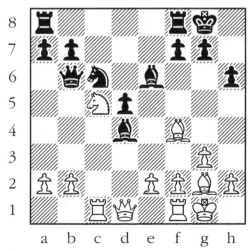

## 221.
### *White to move*
(Mating attack)

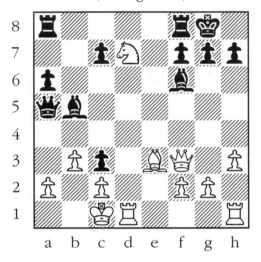

## 222.
### *Black to move*
(Skewer)

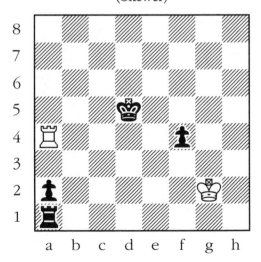

## 223.
### *White to move*
(En prise)

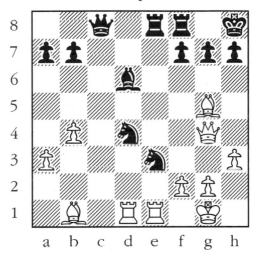

## 224.
### *White to move*
(Mating attack)

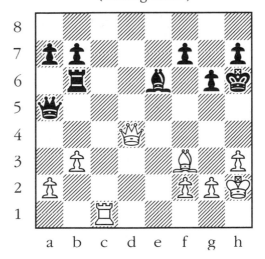

## 225.
### *White to move*
(Promotion)

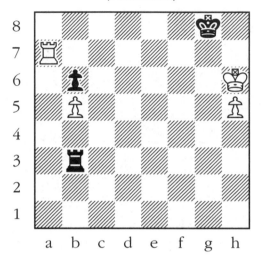

## 226.
### *White to move*
(Back rank)

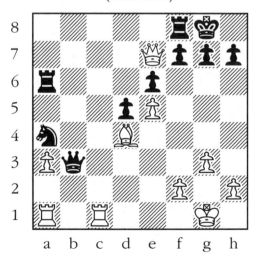

## 227.
### *White to move*
### (Fork)

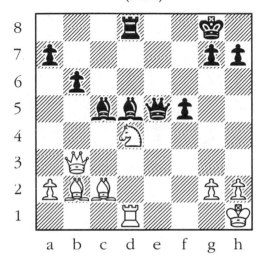

## 228.
### *White to move*
### (Skewer)

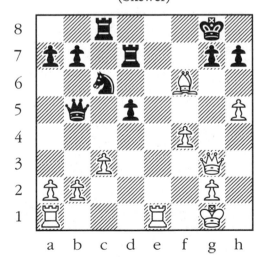

## 229.
### *White to move*
(Infiltration)

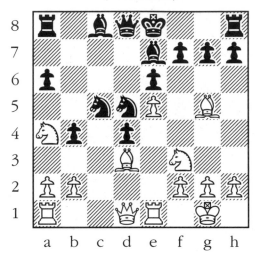

## 230.
### *White to move*
(Driving off)

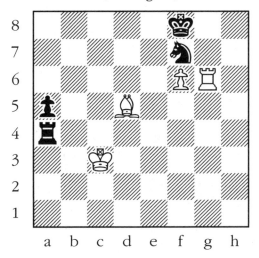

## 231.
### White to move
#### (Removing the guard)

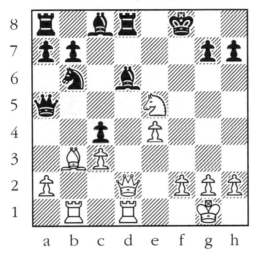

## 232.
### Black to move
#### (Skewer)

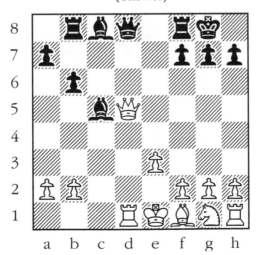

## 233.
### *White to move*
(Driving off)

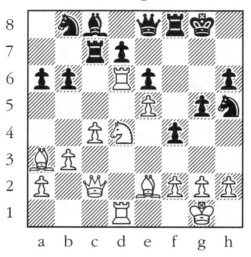

## 234.
### *White to move*
(Mating attack)

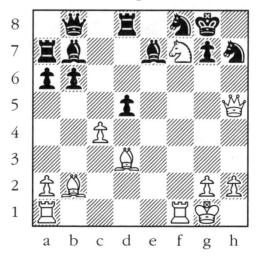

## 235.
### White to move
### (Mating attack)

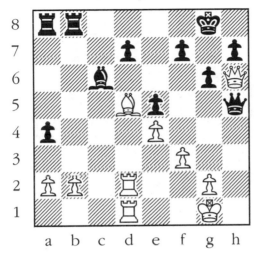

## 236.
### Black to move
### (Removing the guard)

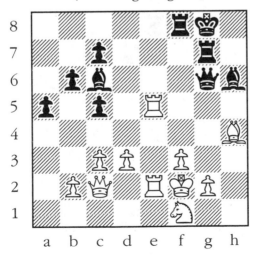

## 237.
### *White to move*
(Mating attack)

## 238.
### *White to move*
(Driving off)

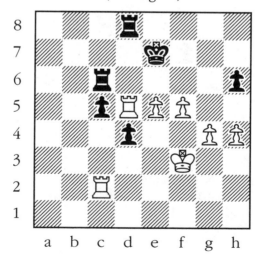

## 239.
### White to move
#### (Pin)

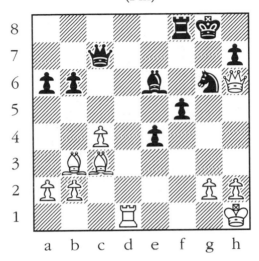

## 240.
### Black to move
#### (Mating attack)

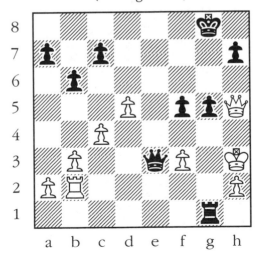

## 241.
### *White to move*
(Removing the guard)

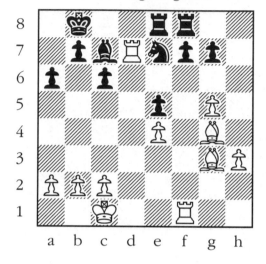

## 242.
### *White to move*
(Removing the guard)

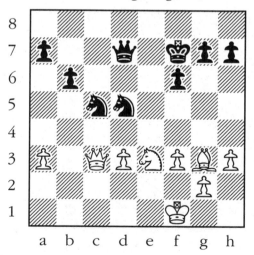

## 243.
### Black to move
(Discovery)

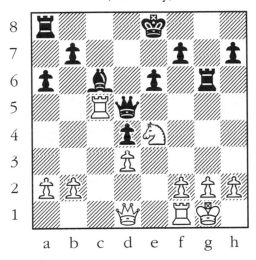

## 244.
### Black to move
(Removing the guard)

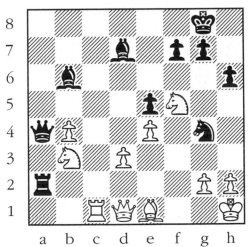

## 245.
### *White to move*
#### (En prise)

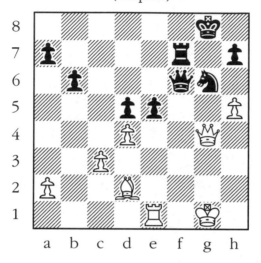

## 246.
### *White to move*
#### (Get out of check)

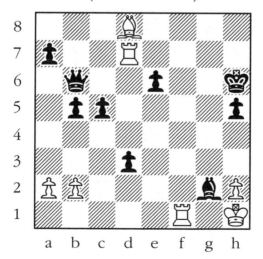

## 247.
### *White to move*
(Driving off)

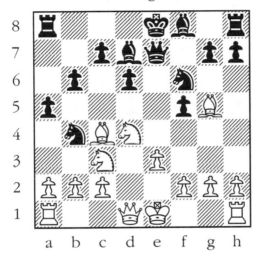

## 248.
### *White to move*
(Overload)

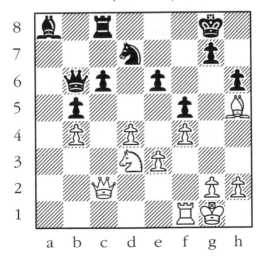

## 249.
### *White to move*
(Back rank)

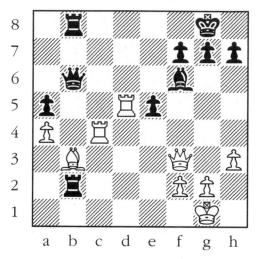

## 250.
### *Black to move*
(Pin/fork)

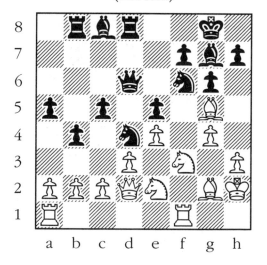

## 251.
### *White to move*
(Discovery)

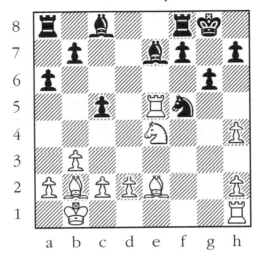

## 252.
### *Black to move*
(Trapping)

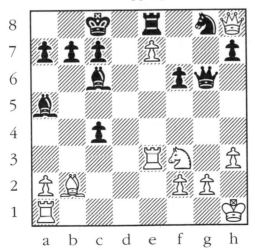

## 253.
### *Black to move*
(En prise)

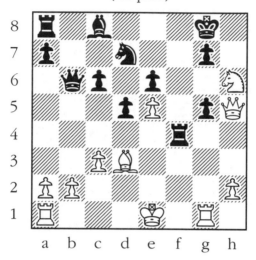

## 254.
### *White to move*
(Discovery)

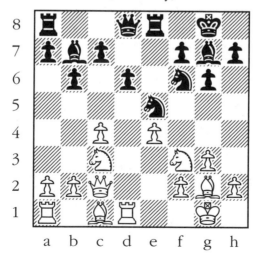

## 255.
### *White to move*
(Mating attack)

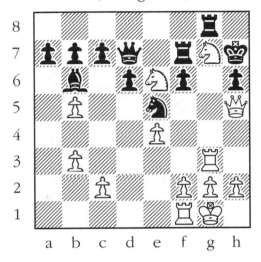

## 256.
### *Black to move*
(Mating attack)

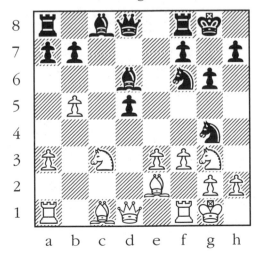

## 257.
### *White to move*
(Mating attack)

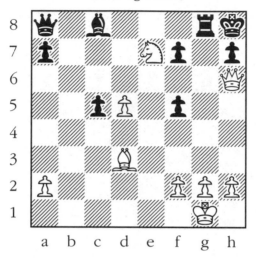

## 258.
### *White to move*
(Mating attack)

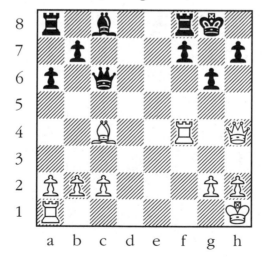

## 259.
### *White to move*
(Skewer)

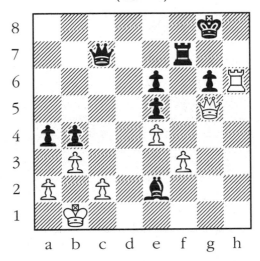

## 260.
### *White to move*
(Mating attack)

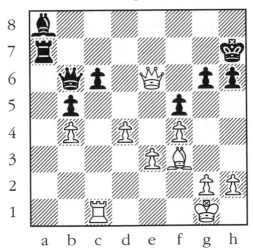

## 261.
### *White to move*
(Mating attack)

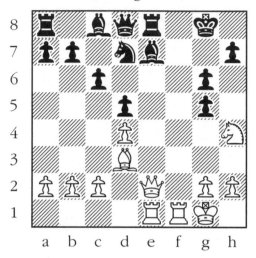

## 262.
### *White to move*
(Mating attack)

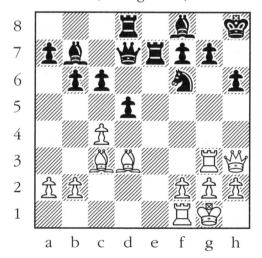

## 263.
### White to move
(Fork)

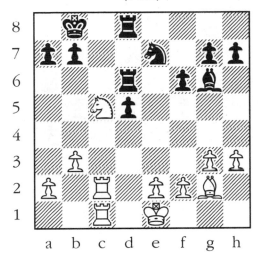

## 264.
### Black to move
(Discovery)

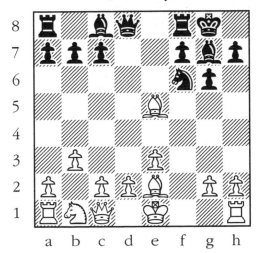

## 265.
### *White to move*
(Promotion)

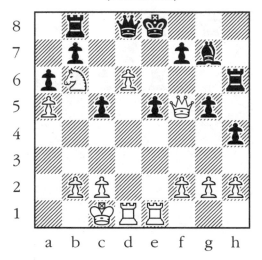

## 266.
### *Black to move*
(Unpin)

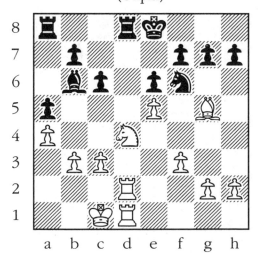

## 267.
### White to move
(Mating attack)

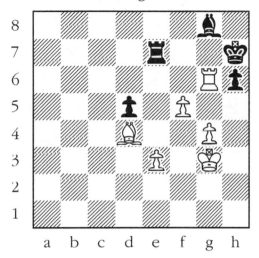

## 268.
### White to move
(Removing the guard)

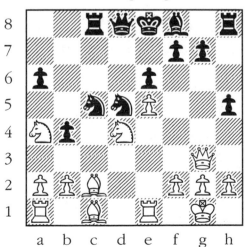

## 269.
### *White to move*
(Pin)

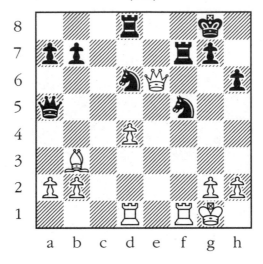

## 270.
### *White to move*
(Discovery)

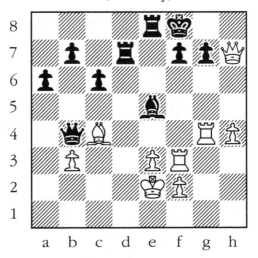

## 271.
### *White to move*
### (Pin)

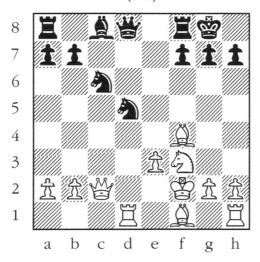

## 272.
### *Black to move*
### (En prise)

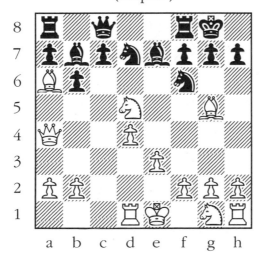

### 273.
*White to move*
(Mating attack)

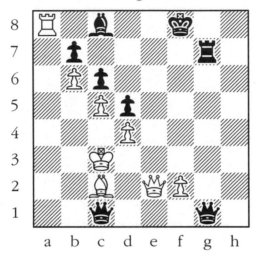

### 274.
*White to move*
(Removing the guard)

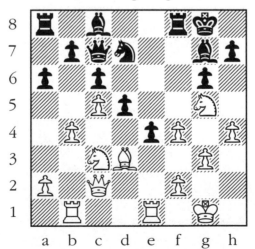

## 275.
### Black to move
#### (Mating attack)

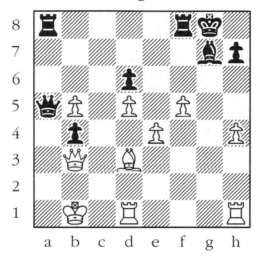

## 276.
### White to move
#### (Mating attack)

## 277.
### *White to move*
(Mating attack)

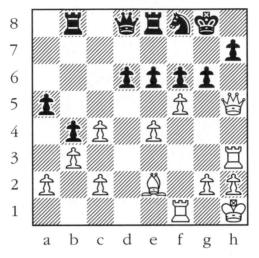

## 278.
### *White to move*
(Removing the guard)

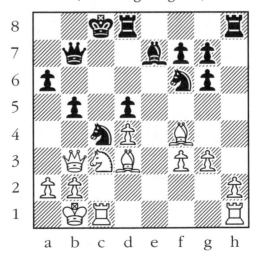

## 279.
### Black to move
(Interference)

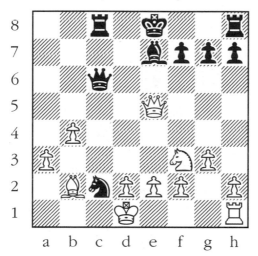

## 280.
### White to move
(Skewer)

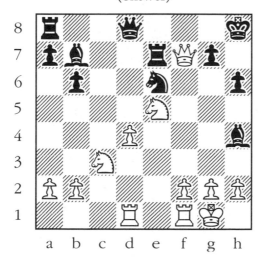

## 281.
### *White to move*
### (Fork)

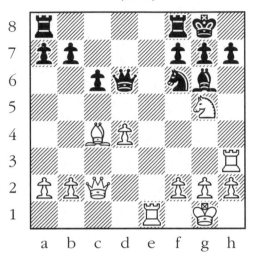

## 282.
### *White to move*
### (Promotion)

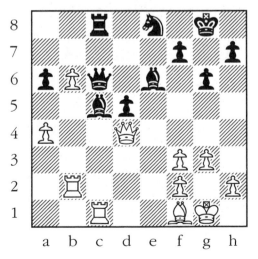

## 283.
### Black to move
### (En prise)

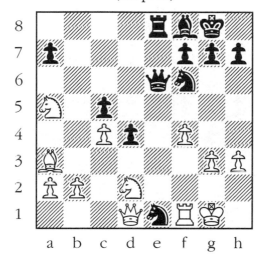

## 284.
### White to move
### (Trapping)

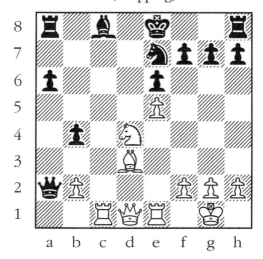

## 285.
### *Black to move*
(Discovery)

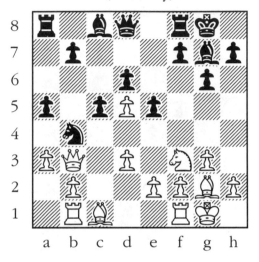

## 286.
### *White to move*
(Promotion)

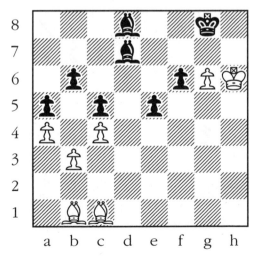

## 287.
### *White to move*
### (Fork)

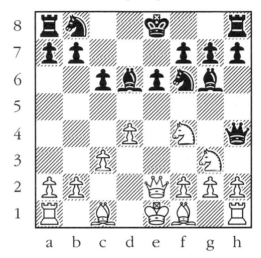

## 288.
### *White to move*
### (Trapping)

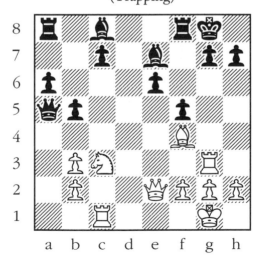

## 289.
### *White to move*
(Mating attack)

## 290.
### *White to move*
(Mating attack)

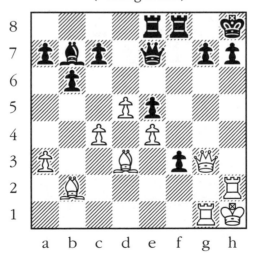

## 291.
### Black to move
### (Overload)

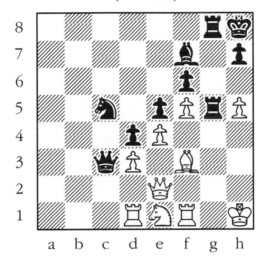

## 292.
### White to move
### (Fork)

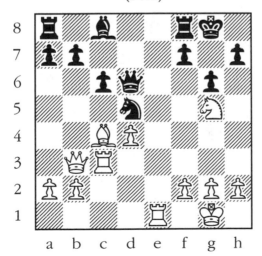

## 293.
### Black to move
(Fork)

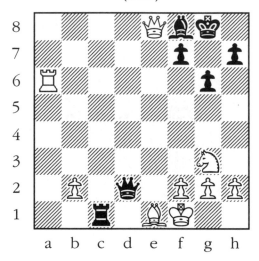

## 294.
### Black to move
(Pin)

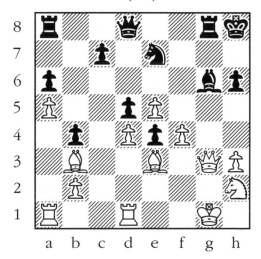

## 295.
### *White to move*
(Discovery)

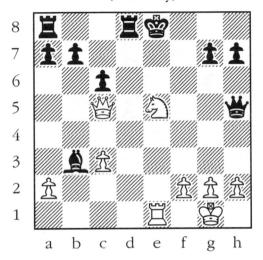

## 296.
### *White to move*
(Removing the guard)

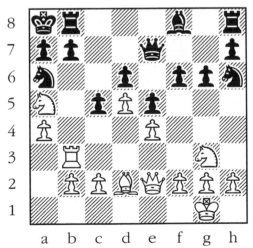

## 297.
### *White to move*
(Driving off)

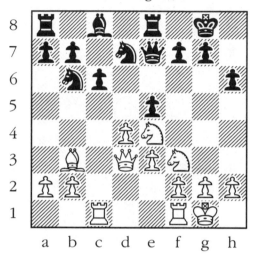

## 298.
### *White to move*
(Mating attack)

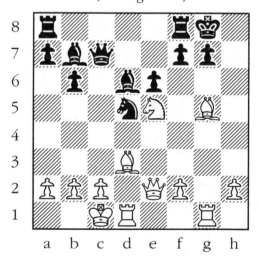

## 299.
### *White to move*
(Removing the guard)

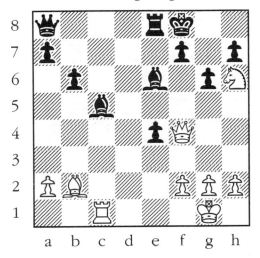

## 300.
### *White to move*
(Mating attack)

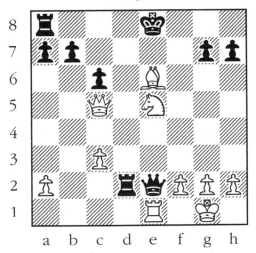

## 300A.
### *White to move*
(Deflection/mating attack)

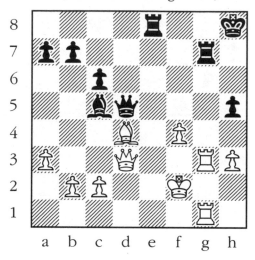

## 300B.
### *Black to move*
(Mating attack)

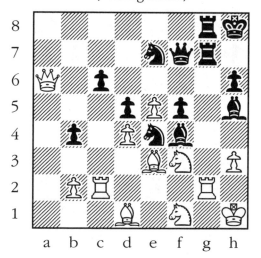

# CHAPTER FOUR
# THE FORK TRICK

## The Fork Trick—Part One
## 301.

*Black to move*

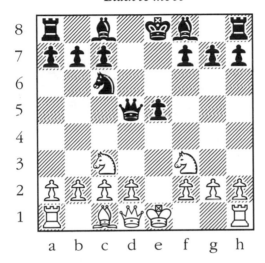

Don't worry if you don't know what the fork trick is; it will be explained when you turn the page. The diagram shows the position a few moves past the fork trick and Black's queen is attacked. The question is where do you put the queen?

There's no single correct answer to this question as several squares beckon. Somewhat reluctantly the author of these lines placed the queen back on her starting square, d8. The deciding factor was a discovery tactic which was in fact realized in the illustrative game. The reader is invited to discover the tactic for himself.

## Illustrative Game #1
### J. Cope – B. Alberston
### Allentown Pa. 1970
### Two Knights Defense

| | | |
|---|---|---|
| 1 | e4 | e5 |
| 2 | Nf3 | Nc6 |
| 3 | Bc4 | Nf6 |

The attack on the e4-pawn can be met in various ways. White can ignore it, 4 d4, 4 Ng5, or he can defend it, 4 Nc3, 4 d3.

| | | |
|---|---|---|
| 4 | Nc3 | Nxe4 |

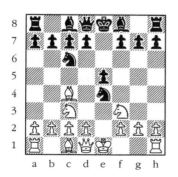

This temporary sacrifice, in conjunction with his next move, constitutes the fork trick. White could have prevented it by selecting 4 d3 on his previous turn.

| | | |
|---|---|---|
| 5 | Nxe4 | d5 |

The fork part of the fork trick. Black recovers his piece and obtains an easy game right out of the opening. In fact, if White is not careful, Black even gets the better of it.

Theory says 6 Bd3 dxe4 7 Bxe4 keeps White on an even keel. However, in the present game White decided to part with his bishop.

| | | |
|---|---|---|
| 6 | Bxd5 | Qxd5 |
| 7 | Nc3 | ... |

Thus we get to the diagram at the head of the chapter. My

first thought was 7 ... Qa5 to be followed by 8 ... Bg4 and queenside castling. There is nothing wrong with this; nevertheless 7 ... Qa5 was rejected. I didn't understand what the queen was supposed to accomplish on a5, nor did I have a ready answer if White played 8 d3 and 9 Bd2.

Another placement was 7 ... Qd6, again, with the idea of ... Bg4 and 0-0-0, and then perhaps sliding the queen to g6. However, 7 ... Qd6 fell by the wayside when I noticed 8 Nb5 forcing the queen back to d8. And I did not intend to return the queen to her starting square. That just seemed stupid.

7 ...          Qd8

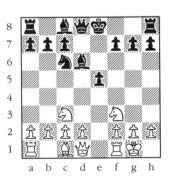

What's this? The queen winds up on d8. How did that

happen? After going through the different queen moves without any tangible result, I took another approach. If Black moves his queen to a different square, what does White want to do?

White's idea seemed pretty clear. He wants to castle and knock out the e5-pawn, which forms the basis of Black's central advantage. So 0-0, Re1, and d4. In turn I have to secure my e-pawn and get my king off the e-line.

At that moment I realized where the queen had to be, on the d-file, not blocking either of my bishops.

8   0-0          Bd6

Black guards his e-pawn in advance and prepares to castle.

9   Re1          0-0

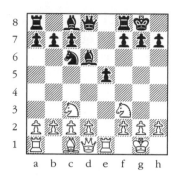

Both sides follow the program mapped out beforehand and now White is ready to advance his d-pawn. One square or two?

**10 d4?        exd4**

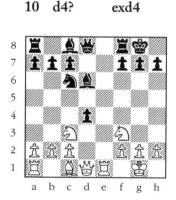

If 11 Nb5 then 10 ... Bg4, White cannot afford to capture at d4 but only comes to realize this at the end.

**11    Nxd4?      Nxd4**
**12    Qxd4?      Bxh2+**

**0-1**

### The Fork Trick—Part Two
**302.**
*Black to move*

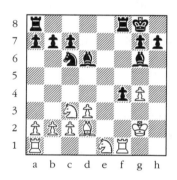

Following the law of averages, the fork trick popped up on my board for the second time in a month. Naturally, in the thirty plus years that followed I never played it again.

In the diagrammed position we're well beyond the moment of the fork trick. Black is a pawn ahead with the better position, so it should be a win and in a couple of ways. Here I very much wanted to play ... Nc6-d4 but needed an answer to Nc3-d5. There's more than one correct reply, which you are invited to find. But I should tell the reader that I'm rather pleased with the one I came up with. It turned out to be totally unexpected, while the calculation took me virtually to the end of the game.

**Illustrative Game #2**
**B. Schmauch – B. Alberston**
**Allentown Pa. 1970**
**Two Knights Defense**

| 1 | e4 | e5 |
|---|------|-------|
| 2 | Nf3 | Nf6 |
| 3 | Nc3 | Nc6 |
| 4 | Bc4 | Nxe4 |
| 5 | Nxe4 | d5 |
| 6 | Bxd5 | Qxd5 |
| 7 | Nc3 | Qd8 |

Following famous precedent, my game earlier in the month. It turns out that 7 ... Qd8 is also the book move but of that precedent I was unaware.

| 8 | d3 | ... |
|---|------|-------|

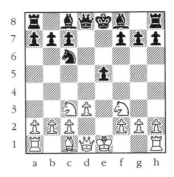

A minor triumph for Black's strategy. The formation Pd3 vs. Pe5 insures Black more center space and the initiative along with it.

| 8 | ... | Bd6 |
|----|------|-------|
| 9 | Be3 | 0-0 |
| 10 | 0-0 | Bg4 |
| 11 | h3 | Bh5 |
| 12 | g4 | Bg6 |

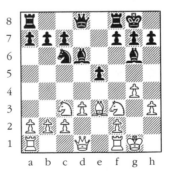

Schmauch has taken the drastic step of advancing his kingside pawns to break the pin. He is probably correct to do so, but his follow up is all wrong.

175

**13 Ne1?** ...

The newly unpinned knight clears a path for the f2-pawn whose advance will further weaken White's kingside. Instead 13 Bg5 f6 14 Bh4 and then Bg3 should have been considered, shoring up the dark squares around White's castled king.

| 13 | ... | f5 |
| 14 | f4 | Qh4 |
| 15 | Kg2 | fxg4 |
| 16 | Qxg4 | Qxg4+ |
| 17 | hxg4 | exf4 |
| 18 | Bd2 | ... |

By trading queens White averted disaster, but along the way he's had to shed a pawn.

Our Part Two heading position. 18 ... Rae8 suggests itself but then 19 Nf3 enables White

to set up stiff resistance. It is in Black's interest to hold the knight at e1 where it interferes with the coordination of the rooks. That means 18 ... Nd4 attacking c2. But then Black needs an answer to 19 Nd5

| 18 | ... | Nd4 |
| 19 | Nd5 | ... |

So what do you do about the f4-pawn? There are at least fives moves to consider.

(1) 19 ... Ne6, instantly rejected on the grounds that there has to be something better. Call it intuition at work.

(2) 19 ... f3+ 20 Nxf3 Nxc2 was possible, as was ...

(3) 19 ... Rae8 20 Nxf4 Bxf4 21 Bxf4 Re2+

These were noticed but not pursued since my attention already was elsewhere.

Not noticed at all and therefore not pursued was …

(4) 19 … Nxc2 20 Nxc2 Bxd3, a line pointed out by one of my students. Second category at the time, student went on to become a master.

**19 …       Bf7**

Line (5). Black is ready to return his extra pawn to open the f-file and activate his light squared bishop. If White had seen what was coming he might have tried 20 c4, but the natural move is to recover the lost pawn.

**20 Nxf4       g5**

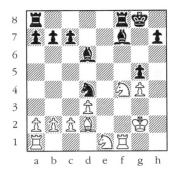

This is why I like my combination. It's not obvious from the previous diagrams that the g7-pawn has a role to play. If 21 Be3 the intention was 21 … Bxf4 22 Bxd4 Be6 and the g4-pawn is untenable: 23 Kh3 h5.

**21 c3       Bxf4**
**22 Bxf4       Bd5+**

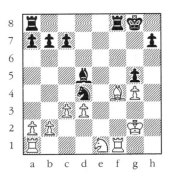

**23 Nf3**

A short circuit in a lost position. I expected 23 Kh2 (23 Kg1 Ne2+) 23 … Ne6 winning the pinned bishop. Here is where the disconnect between the White rooks tells.

**23 …       Nxf3**
**24 Rxf3       Rxf4**
**25 Rf1       Rxf3**

0-1

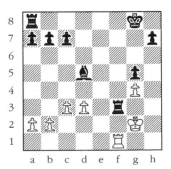

## The Fork Trick—Part Three
### 303.
*Black to move*

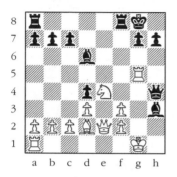

The diagram position comes from the game D.J. Hermann versus Rudolf Charousek, Budapest, 1896. Black has broken up the White castled position and now the task is to finish off the king. If you can't get the king, then at least get the queen. That will be sufficient. See if you can figure out how the brilliant Hungarian wrapped up his victory.

The significance of Hermann-Charousek is that it forms a precedent in the openings discussion of the fork trick. Carl Schlechter noted the game and placed it into the 8th edition of *Bilguer's Handbuch*. English speaking readers can find it in Sergeant's collection of Charousek's games.

## Illustrative Game #3
### D.J. Hermann – R. Charousek
### Budapest 1896
### Two Knights Defense

| 1 | e4 | e5 |
|---|-----|------|
| 2 | Nf3 | Nc6 |
| 3 | Bc4 | Nf6 |
| 4 | Nc3 | Nxe4 |
| 5 | Nxe4 | d5 |
| 6 | Bxd5 | Qxd5 |
| 7 | Nc3 | Qd8 |

So now we know where 7 ... Qd8 really came from. I always thought it was from a 1970 Alberston game.

| 8 | 0-0 | Bd6 |
|---|-----|------|
| 9 | d3 | 0-0 |
| 10 | h3 | ... |

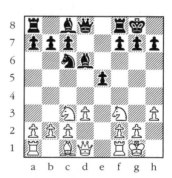

To prevent ... Bg4. Later on the h3-pawn becomes a target, but these things can't always be helped. 10 Ne1

intending 11 f4 is an untested suggestion.

**10 ...    f5**

Black is the first to advance his f-pawn, gaining kingside space. Should White at some point push in the center d3-d4, Black can safely move past, ... e5-e4, hitting the f3-Knight.

**11  Re1    Bd7**
**12  Qe2    Qe8**
**13  Be3    Qg6**

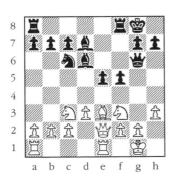

Charousek steadily builds his kingside assault, already threatening 14 ... f4 followed by 15 ... Bxh3. This prompts White to remove his king from the g-file.

**14  Kh1    f4**
**15  Bd2    Nd4**

To eliminate the defending f3-Knight.

**16  Nxd4    ...**

Taking 16 Nxe5, is bad. Black has 16 ... Qf5, also 16 ... Bxe5 17 Qxe5 Nxc2 winning material. So, White agrees to the trade of knights. In retrospect 16 Qd1 looks like the safer move.

**16  ...    exd4**
**17  Ne4    f3!**

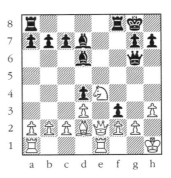

Forces a breach in the castled position and causes real problems. The best defense is 18 Qf1. What he plays doesn't help.

**18  gxf3    Bxh3**
**19  Rg1    ...**

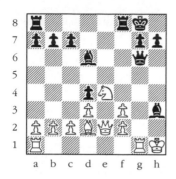

Stops mate but now the king is jammed up. Charousek goes about setting up discovered check on the h-file.

| 19 | ... | Qh5 |
| 20 | Rg5 | ... |

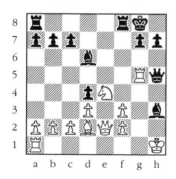

| 20 | ... | Qh4 |
| 21 | Kg1 | ... |

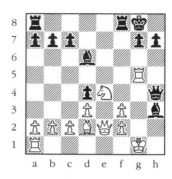

See if you can figure out the pretty finish.

| 21 | ... | Bh2+! |
| 22 | Kh1 | ... |

If he takes the bishop 22 Kxh2, then of course 22 ... Bf1+ wins the queen. So the king ends up back in the corner.

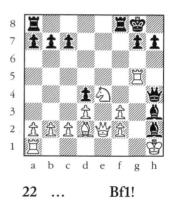

| 22 | ... | Bf1! |

Anyway! If he takes the bishop, 23 Rxf1, he blocks the king's exit, and it's mate in two

by 23 ... Bg3+ and 24 ...
Qh2#. He can take with the
queen, 23 Qxf1, but then to
avoid mate, he has to dump the
queen at h3.

**23   Qd1      ...**

23 Qe1 makes no differ-
ence. Black still plays the same
move.

**23   ...        Be2!**

**0-1**

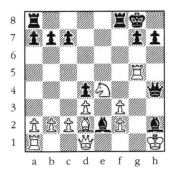

After 24 Qxe2 the escape is
once again blocked: 24 ...
Bg3+ 25 Kg2 Qh2+ 26 Kf1
Qh1#. Not a bad game for an
opening precedent.

## The Fork Trick—Part Four
## 304.

*Black to move*

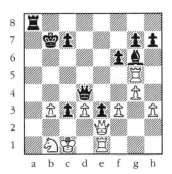

You should realize by now
that our book is lopsided.
Well, it's supposed to be lopsided. It's all about tactics with
no mention of strategic play. In
this last part we redress the
balance, even if ever so slightly,
by presenting an unknown
strategic masterpiece by Carl
Schlechter. As editor of the
8th edition, he slipped it into
the *Handbuch* right behind the
Charousek game. It's buried
inside a column and a footnote.

Of course there are some
tactics sprinkled in and our
diagrammed position is toward
the end of the game. So how
did Schlechter finish up? Inci-
dentally, in the opening,
Schlecter played 7 ... Qa5, not
7 ... Qd8.

## Illustrative Game #4
### A. Schwartz – C. Schlechter
### Vienna 1897-98
### Two Knights Defense

| | | |
|---|---|---|
| 1 | e4 | e5 |
| 2 | Nf3 | Nc6 |
| 3 | Bc4 | Nf6 |
| 4 | Nc3 | Nxe4 |
| 5 | Nxe5 | d5 |
| 6 | Bxd5 | Qxd5 |
| 7 | Nc3 | Qa5 |

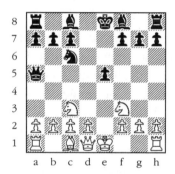

As we know from part one, Alberston considered this queen move but then decided against it. On a5 the queen is exposed to further attack and will have to move again. Overuse of the queen? Maybe, but for Schlechter this was not a problem.

| 8 | d3 | ... |

This has to be played directly for if White dallies, 8 h3, to prevent ... Bg4, then 8 ... Bb4 and the d-pawn can't move.

| 8 | ... | Bg4 |

Threatens 9 ... Nd4 and takes on f3, busting up White's pawns. So like it or not, White has to forcibly break the pin.

| 9 | h3 | Bh5 |
| 10 | g4 | Bg6 |
| 11 | Bd2 | Bb4 |
| 12 | a3 | Bxc3 |
| 13 | Bxc3 | Qd5 |

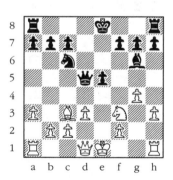

The problem of where to put the queen is solved. She's back on d5, an excellent post from which she cannot easily be dislodged.

| 14 | Qe2 | ... |

Having advanced the king-side pawns, 0-0 is out of the question. So White makes preparations to castle queen-side, although here too the king is not completely secure.

14 ...         0-0-0
15 0-0-0     ...

This looks dangerous as ... Qa2 is in the air. Presumably White intended to answer Nf3-d2-b1 (as later in the game). In any event Schlechter is in no rush. First he finishes off his development, with a threat.

15 ...         Rhe8

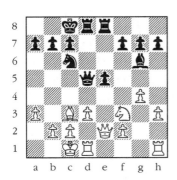

Now there are a number of unpleasantries in the air: 16 ... Qa2, 16 ... e4, but mainly 16 ... Nd4 17 B(N)xd4 exd4 when Black wins a piece. White's next is probably his only move.

16 Nd2       b5!

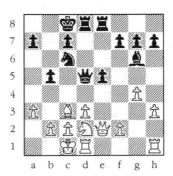

They tell you not to move the pawns around your king, but there are always exceptions, which the good players seem to find. Here Black's superior control of the board precludes White from developing any attack worthy of the name. And the advance of the b-pawn is the first line in the attack against the White's castled king. The pawn structure has to be softened up.

17 f3         ...

To shore up e4 after the knight moves from d2 so there's no easy breakthrough in the center with ... e5-e4.

17 ...         a5

The threat to trap the bishop ( … b4) forces a breach in king's fortress which Black immediately fastens onto.

**18  b3        Qc5**

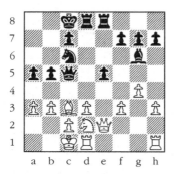

A change of front. The queen can no longer break in at a2 so she threatens both the bishop and the a3-pawn. 19 Kb2 won't do because of 19 … b4, trapping the bishop. And 19 Bb2 fails to 19 … Bxd3, thanks to the newly pinned c2-pawn. White's next move is forced.

**19  Nb1      f6**

Pure unhurried Schlechter. Before getting down to business he calmly secures his position in the center. He knows that White cannot improve his position in any significant way,

and given a little rope he might easily make it worse.

**20  Rhf1      …**

In order to challenge the Black queen with 21 Qf2.

**20  …        b4**
**21  axb4      axb4**

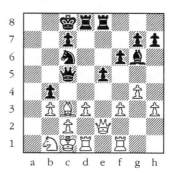

**22  Ba1      …**

A strange looking retreat; one expects 22 Bb2. But Schwartz, to his credit, realizes that 22 Bb2 fails against 22 … Na5! threatening nothing less than 23 … Nxb3#. The king would have to step up 23 Kd2 and that would invite the central breakthrough 23 … e4, with all sorts of brilliant sacrifices. The withdrawal to a1 allows 22 … Na5 to be answered with 23 Kb2.

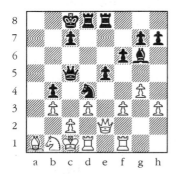

Threatens e2, c2, and b3. The knight has to be captured after which Black obtains an open e-file for his rook along with an outpost at e3. Further, White's defenses on the dark squares grows weaker, after his bishop disappears.

| 23 | Bxd4 | exd4 |
|----|------|------|
| 24 | Qf2  | Re3  |

Ganging up on the d3-pawn, 25 ... Bxd3. The king has to shelter on the b-file to unpin the c2-pawn.

| 25 | Kb2 | Kb7 |
|----|-----|-----|

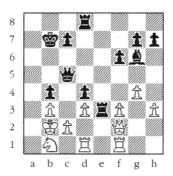

Symmetrical king moves, but with a huge difference. White's is strictly defensive, while Black's is offensive, making room for his rook to reach the a-file.

| 26 | Rfe1 | Ra8  |
|----|------|------|
| 27 | Rxe3 | dxe3 |

The exchange of rooks has not eased the defense. Black's has been replaced by an intrusive pawn.

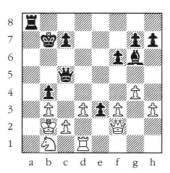

185

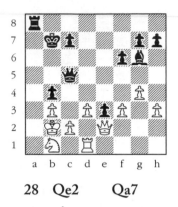

**28 Qe2        Qa7**

Marvelous restraint. Most players could hardly resist the check at d4 especially since it looks pretty strong:

28 ... Qd4+ 29 c3 (29 Kc1 Ra2) 29 ... bxc3+ 30 Nxc3 Ra6 with 31 ... Rc6.

Schlechter fully intends to bring his queen to d4, but without allowing c2-c3. His idea is 29 ... Qa1+ 30 Kc1 Qd4 and then 31 ... Ra2 (or Ra1) as circumstances dictate.

**29 Kc1        Qd4**

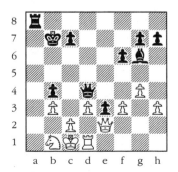

The queen's on d4 and there's nothing much White can do about it. If 30 Re1 Ra2 31 Qxe3 Qb2+ and 32 ... Qxc2#. The only way to defend the second rank is to move the c-pawn, but now Black just takes it off for nothing.

**30 c4         bxc3 e.p.**
**31 Re1        ...**

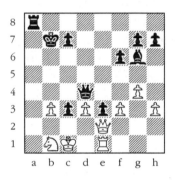

The diagram at the beginning of Part Four. White hopes that Black will take the d3-pawn: 31 ... Qxd3 32 Qxd3 Bxd3 33 Rxe3, or perhaps 31 ... Bxd3 32 Rd1. And if he doesn't take the pawn then maybe White will have time to take the e3-pawn.

**31 ...         Ra1!**

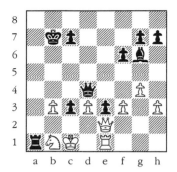

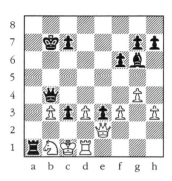

Leaving no time for 32 Qxe3 because of 32 ... Bxd3 33 Qxd4 Rxb1 mate.

**32 Rd1    Qb4**

**0-1**

No defense against 33 ... Qa3+ 34 Kc2 Qb2#. If 33 Kc2 then 33 ... Ra2+ skewers the queen.

We've labeled this game a strategic masterpiece (perhaps a bit overblown) and then proceeded to call your attention to all the hidden tactical points. Well, that's just the way it is. You can't have one without the other.

# CHAPTER FIVE
## DEFLECTION, UNDERMINING, OR REMOVING THE GUARD?

### 305.

*White to move*

We have noticed over the years a surprising lack of consensus among chess teachers, chess authors—indeed chess players in general—regarding definitions of standard tactical themes. For example, we all know (or should know), that a *fork* and a *double attack* are essentially the same thing. When this attack on two units simultaneously by a single man is carried out by a knight or a pawn we usually call this tactic a *fork*. However, when this tactic effected by a bishop, rook or queen we usually call it a *double attack*!

Also, we have found a surprising lack of consistency within the chess community when discussing the extremely important tactic involving removing or eliminating a defender. We have most often found this kind of tactic described as either *deflection*, *undermining*, or *removing the guard*, with about equal frequency. Fred Reinfeld in his classic *1001 Brilliant Chess Sacrifices and*

*Combinations* (1955), when discussing *removing the guard*, points out that "... the principle underlying this theme is the very essence of chess logic. If Piece A guards Piece B, attack Piece A and you win one or the other." He further adds that "removing the guard is one of the most useful of all the tactical themes. In chess, there is no surer winning method than concentrating on hostile units that are tied down to some vital task." Later on, in *Pandolfini's Chess Complete* (1992), our friend Bruce defines *removing the defender* as "a tactic making a unit vulnerable by capturing, luring or driving away, or immobilizing its protector. Also called removing the guard or undermining." And in Patrick Wolf's superb *The Complete Idiot's Guide to Chess* (1995), he states "deflection refers to when one piece is forced to move away from a square where it is needed for some reason." Interestingly, M.V. Blokh, in his famous masterpiece about chess tactics, *The Art of Combination* (1994), uses none of the three most common ways for describing *removing the defender* but instead refers to this concept by the fearsome phrase *annihilation of defense*.

While we could give countless examples, we think you get the idea—there is no agreement among chess writers regarding standard definitions of many fundamental tactical concepts. No matter what you would call this tactical operation—*deflection, undermining,* or *removing the guard*—we would add to its definitions that *to carry it out successfully, you must eliminate your opponent's control of a square vital to his safety.*

The position at the beginning of this chapter (Diagram 305) is the last, and perhaps most difficult combination to solve in this book. It is not so hard because of its length but rather because of the difficulty in discerning what square in Black's position White needs to undermine. Fred discovered this virtually unknown masterpiece while browsing through the August 1965 issue of *Chess Review*, a great periodical that ran from 1933 to 1969. We know of no electronic databases nor published game collections that contain the following brilliancy by International Master Walter Shipman (who is still an active force on the California chess scene).

**Walter Shipman (Manhattan Chess Club) – Louis Levy (Marshall Chess Club)
New York City, Metropolitan Chess League, 1965
Scandinavian Defense**

**1 e4    d5**

Also known as the *Center Counter Defense*, which while no longer used much by top grandmasters, is extremely popular with amateurs who like dynamic piece activity.

**2  exd5    Qxd5
3  Nc3     Qa5
4  d4      Nf6
5  Bc4     c6
6  Nge2(!)**

White's standard move is 6 Nf3 which leads to several long, deeply analyzed variations that are quite complex.

We are here recommending a little-known sideline which is generally neglected or even completely ignored by current opening literature. In fact, in his otherwise excellent *The Scandinavian* (1997), John Emms only mentions an analogous position from the game Yudasin-Oll, Dos Hermanas, 1992 which went 1 e4 d5 2 exd5 Qxd5 3 Nc3 Qa5 4 Bc4 Nf6 5 d4 Bg4 6 f3 Bf5 7 Nge2 c6 8 g4 Bg6 9 Nf4 Nbd7 10 h4 e5 11 h5! Bf5 12 gxf5 exf4 13 Qd3 Qc7 14 Qe2+ Be7 15 Bd2 Nb6 16 Bb3 Rd8 17 0-0-0! with White having a strong attack which eventually succeeded.

**6 ...    e6**

For the apparently more active 6 ... Bf5, see the supplemental game Kristol-Morozova that follows this one. Apparently, Levy, a strong master, carefully examined Black's potential problems after 7 Ng3, followed by an early advance of White's f-pawn and decided to "play it safe." Although he does achieve a position akin to the solid Caro

Kann defense, we believe Black has lost time with his queen and should be slightly worse. In fact, Shipman now, with a simple developing move, takes away Black's best square for his queen (c7).

| 7 | Bf4! | Nbd7 |
|---|------|------|
| 8 | 0-0  | Be7  |
| 9 | Qd2! |      |

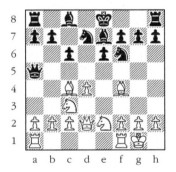

Shipman sets a nice trap. After the apparently safe 9 … 0-0 10 Nd5! Qd8 11 Nxe7 Qxe7 12 Bg5. White has a clear advantage.

| 9 | … | Qb4 |
|---|---|-----|

Hans Kmoch, in *Chess Review* (August 1965), observes that "Black's queen remains awkwardly placed for the remainder of the game.

Still, the 'safe' 9 … Qd8 is not very appetizing either."

| 10 | Bb3  | 0-0  |
|----|------|------|
| 11 | Rad1 | Bd6  |
| 12 | Rfe1 | Bxf4 |
| 13 | Qxf4 | Nb6  |
| 14 | Rd3  | Nbd5 |

Black is attempting to bring more pieces to his King side as White is clearly gearing up for a strong attack.

| 15 | Qh4   | Ne7  |
|----|-------|------|
| 16 | Ng3   | Ng6  |
| 17 | Qg5   | h6   |
| 18 | Qd2   | Bd7  |
| 19 | Nce4! |      |

As Kmoch notes, "… the endgame, after 19 … Qxd2 20 Nxf6+ gxf6 21 Rxd2 f5 22 Nh5 favors White. Still, Black ought to take it on as the middle game is perilous for him." Indeed, we believe it was essential for Levy to trade queens, although even in 1965, facing Walter Shipman in a long, difficult endgame was quite a thankless task. What Levy does here, chessically, is "jumping out of the frying pan and into the fire."

| 19 | ... | Nd5? |
| 20 | c3 | Qa5? |

Although 20 ... Qe7 was imperative, after 20 Nc5, threatening 21 Nf5, Black's position is terrible. What now follows is a wonderful combination and a terrific example of removing the guard ... but for what square? See if you can figure it out.

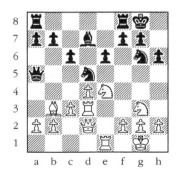

| 21 | Bxd5!! | exd5 |

Kmoch points out that "21 ... cxd5 makes no difference; and, on 21 ... Qxd5, White gets the same combination after 24 c4! Qxc4 (forced)."

| 22 | Nf6+! | gxf6 |
| 23 | Qxh6 | |

And now you know what Black square White needed to conquer!

| 23 | ... | Rfe8(?) |

If 23 ... Bg4 24 h3 Qc7 aiming for a possible queen trade if 25 hxg4 Qf4, White is forced to find 25 Rf3! Bxf3 26 Nf5.

| 24 | Rf1! | Resigns |

For if 24 ... Bg4 25 f3 Qc7 26 fxg4 forces mate or wins Black's queen for a knight.

## SUPPLEMENTAL GAME

(A trenchant example of the problems Black might face if he plays 6 ... Bf5 in this variation)

### L. Kristol – T. Morozova
### Scandinavian Defense
### Soviet Union, 1966

1 e4 d5 2 exd5 Qxd5 3 Nc3 Qa5 4 d4 Nf6 5 Bc4 c6 6 Nge2(!) Bf5 7 0-0 e6 8 Ng3 Bg6 9 Qe2 Be7 10 f4! Qd8 (if 10 ... 0-0?? 11 f5 wins a bishop) 11 f5! exf5 12 Nxf5 Bxf5 13 Rxf5 Qxd4+?? (An astonishingly greedy mistake! As Black will lose the right to castle and is way behind in development, this is simply suicidal. Black had to play 13 ... 0-0, when after 14 Be3, White, with his two bishops and greater central control, is clearly better.) 14 Be3 Qd7 15 Bc5 Kf8 (forced) 16 Rd1 Bxc5+ 17 Rxc5 Qc7 (Notice White has five pieces developed against Black's two, plus Black has also forfeited castling—certainly these advantages are worth much more than one pawn.) 18 Re5 Na6 19 Re1 b5 20 Re7! Qb6+ 21 Kh1 bxc4 22 Qxc4 Nd5 23 Nxd5 Qb5

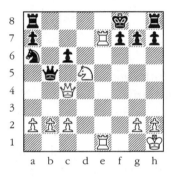

**24 Nf6!      Resigns.**

Mate in two moves cannot be stopped. 24 Nc7! is the same thing. A cautionary tale!

# ANSWERS

**1.**

1 Re7 with unstoppable mate.

**2.**

1 h3 Qxg2 2 Rh2 or 1 ...
Qf5(h5) 2 g4.

**3.**

1 Nd5 Rf8 2 Nf4
overpowering g6.

**4.**

1 ... Rd1+ 2 Kxd1 Qxe5.

**5.**

1 Rf8+ Kxf8 2 Qf7#.

**6.**

1 Nxf7+ (a) 1 ... Rxf7 2 Rxe6
(b) 2 ... Bxf7 3 Rd6 pins the
queen.

**7.**

1 Successful promotion turns
on an in-between-check 1
Qf5+ (a) 1 ... Kg7 2 fxe8/N+
(b) 1 ... Kh8 2 fxe8/Q.

**8.**

1 Qxc3 Rxc3 2 Ne7#.

**9.**

1 Bg7 and queen mates at h7
or h8.

**10.**

1 d4 threatens 2 Rf3 to catch
the enemy queen. So Black
will give a piece by 1 ... Bxd4
2 Nxd4 Qxc3 etc.

**11.**

1 ... Re1+ 2 Kg2 Re2 gets the
nod over 1 ... Re2 2 Re4 as 2
... Rxe4 3 fxe4 Qxe4+ wins
only a pawn or two.

**12.**

1 ... Re1 wins against any
White reply.

**13.**

1 Rxb6 axb6 2 Nf6+ wins the
black queen.

**14.**

1 Qxh7+ Kxh7 2 hxg6#.

**15.**

1 Rxg7+ Kh8 2 Rxh7#.

## 16.

1 Rxe6 gains the bishop for if
1 … Qxe6 2 Ng5 mates or
wins the queen.

## 17.

1 Qh8+ Kxh8 2 Rxf8#.

## 18.

1 b5 drives the knight from
defense of a7.

## 19.

1 Nh6 discovers on the bishop
and the e5-pawn. There's no
defense.

## 20.

1 Qa2+ and if 1 … Kf8 2
Nh7# or 2Qf7#.

## 21.

1 Rb8 and promotes or else 1
… Rxa7 2 Rb5 mates.

## 22.

1 Kxa3? Kxc5, and 1 bxa3?
leaves White with the wrong
colored rook's pawn. So by
elimination, 1 b3 Kd5 2 Bf8
and wins the endgame.

## 23.

1 Rxe7 Rxe7 2 Bc5 wins a
piece.

## 24.

1 … Re1+ 2 Rxe1 (2 Kh2
Qh1#) 2 … Qxd3.

## 25.

1 Bxg6 and Black's game is
resignable. (a) 1 … hxg6 2
Qh8# (b) 1 … fxg6 2 Qe6+
Rf7 3 Qxf7#.

## 26.

1 Bxg7 Kxg7 2 f5 wins the
light squared bishop.

## 27.

1 Rbc1 when Black loses at
least a piece. He has too many
guys en prise.

## 28.

Black draws by keeping the
enemy king confined to g8.
1 … Rh2 temporizing. If
2 Rb7+ Ke8 3 Rf7 Rh1, etc.
White is unable to make any
progress. There may be other
ways to draw but this is by far
the simplest.

## 29.

1 … Nxe2+ 2 Nxe2 Bxb2.

**30.**

1 e3 Nxe3 2 Re1 wins something. Two pins is too much.

**31.**

1 Qxg4 hxg4 2 Ne6#.

**32.**

1 Qe7+ Qf7 2 f6#.

**33.**

1 Qxc6+ wins at least a piece for if 1 ... bxc6 or 1 ... Qxc6 2 Rd8#.

**34.**

1 Qe6+ and 2 Qxc6.

**35.**

1 ... Bxg3 picks off a free pawn.

**36.**

1 ... Rxb1 2 Rxb1 Nxc2 pilfers a pawn.

**37.**

1 Qd4 mates on g7 or else wins the knight.

**38.**

1 Rxf5 Rxf5 2 Bxa8 makes off with a knight.

**39.**

1 Ne5 and nothing can prevent a quick mate when White's queen gets to f6.

**40.**

After 1 Ba3 threatening Bxc5, Black cannot escape material loss. If 1 ... Nd3 2 Bxf8 is sufficient.

**41.**

1 Be6 Qe7 2 d5+ wins the exchange after 2 ... Rf6.

**42.**

1 Qh3+ forces resignation. Our fellow teacher Jonathan Phanstiel's coolest mate in 2003.

**43.**

1 Be7 wins on the spot as 1 ... Nxe7 allows 2 Bxe6+, and if 1 ... Qxe7 2 Qh7+ Kf8 3 Qh8#. Black's queen has been deflected into blocking her king's escape square.

**44.**

1 ... Nxb3 wins a pawn; 2 Qxb3? Rb7 gets the queen.

## 45.

1 Nxd5 threatens 2 Nxb6 or 2 Qxc8+ and comes away with a pawn.

## 46.

1 ... Qh6 with threats of 2 ... Qxc1+ or 2 ... Qh3+ gets the Black queen out of pin.

## 47.

1 Rg3 to stop ... Qf4+. Then nothing stops Qf8 along with Qg7#.

## 48.

1 Rc7 Qd6 (1 ... Qxc7 2 Ne6+) 2 Rxb7, and if 2 ... exf4 3 Qe8+ etc.

## 49.

1 ... Qh1 2 Ng1 Nh2#.

## 50.

1 Nxd6+ wins a pawn as 1 ... Qxd6? drops the queen to 2 Bb5+.

## 51.

1 Rg5+ Kh8 (1 ... fxg5 2 Qxc6) 2 Rg7 forces mate.

## 52.

1 ... Rc1+ 2 Qxc1 (2 Ka2 Ra1#) 2 ... Nxc1 3 Kxc1 leaves Black two pawns up in the endgame.

## 53.

1 Bxg6 hxg6 2 h5 and Black can't stop both the b and h pawns. The same goes for 1 ... h6 2 g5 hxg5 3 h5. One way or another a pawn breaks through.

## 54.

1 Rxc6+ bxc6 2 Nc5 Rhd8 3 Ba6+.

## 55.

Already a pawn down, White faces loss of a piece (enemy pawn fork at e4). He can just escape by 1 Bxa6 and if 1 ... dxf3 2 Bf1.

## 56.

1 ... Nxe2+ 2 Qxe2 is satisfactory for White. So, 1 ... Qxf6 2 gxf3 Qxf3 and Black comes out ahead.

## 57.

1 ... Qxf1+ 2 Kxf1 Rc1+ 3 Ke2 Rb2+ and mate next.

## 58.

1 ... Rxg2+ 2 Kxg2 Bxe3.
Two pieces are normally
better than a rook.

## 59.

1 ... Nxe5, gains a pawn and
introduces another Black
attacker into the frame. The
threat is 2 ... Nf3+ 3 Kf1
Nd2+ 4 Ke1 Rf1#.

## 60.

1 Bc5 Q-moves 2. Bxf8 nabs
the exchange.

## 61.

1 ... Nxd4 2 exd4 Bxf5 puts
Black a full piece ahead.

## 62.

1 ... Bf7+ (a) Nc4 Rxc4, (b) 2
b3 Rc2+, (c) 2 Ka3 Ra1+ or 2
... Nb5+.

## 63.

1 Rxa7+ Kxa7 2 Rxc7+ Ka8 3
Nxb6#.

## 64.

1 ... Ba6 saves the bishop and
threatens 2 ... Rf1+. White
could try 2 Rc8 Bxc8 3 Bxc8
but after 3 ... Qf5, he's still
losing.

## 65.

1 ... Nxd4 wins a pawn, but 1
... Ne5 is even better.

## 66.

1 ... Bxd4+ and 2 ... Bxa1
looks to be the cleanest. If 2
Ne3 then 2 ... hxg5.

## 67.

1 ... Bb5 2 Re1 Rd8 and the
knight falls.

## 68.

1 Rgxf6+ Rxf6 2 Qxg7#.

## 69.

1 ... Rg6, along with 2 ...
Rh8 (mate threat) wins the
queen. So does 1 ... Rg4, but
things get a bit sticky after 2
Qxg4 fxg4 3 Kg3 Rg8 4 Rh7+
etc.

## 70.

1 Bxf6 Bxf6 2 Rxd7.

## 71.

1 ... Nxd4 2 exd4 Nf3+, and 3
... Nxd4, gains a pawn.

## 72.

1 Bxf5 Qxf5 2 Qxh6+ gxh6 3
Rhxh6#.

### 73.

1 Bxc6 and 2 Nxe5 wins a pawn.

### 74.

1 ... dxe4 gains another pawn owing to the attack on the queen; 2 fxe4? Qxd4. And if 2 Qxd8 Raxd8 3 fxe4 Nxe4.

### 75.

1 ... Bxe3 2 Nxe3 Rxh2#. The knight is pinned against the h2-square.

### 76.

1 ... Ne3 2 Rxd2 Nxf1+, and 3 ... Nxd2. If 2 Rb1 Nxf1+ 3 Rxf1 Rxd3 and White is two pawns down.

### 77.

1 Rxa4 wins a pawn as Black cannot afford to take. If 1 ... Rxa4 2 Qxd8+; and if 1 ... Rxd4 2 Rxa8+.

### 78.

1 ... Nxd4+ 2 exd4 Qf3+ etc.

### 79.

1 ... Rxd4 wins a knight for if 2 exd4 Qe1+ forces mate.

### 80.

1 ... Qxd2, but not 1 ... Bxd2 2 h4 Qf4 3 g3 pushing the queen away from the bishop.

### 81.

1 Qxc7+ forces mate.

### 82.

1 Be6 wins the house, e.g., if 1 ... Nxh1 2 Bxd7+ Bxd7 3 Nh3 and Black's knight can't escape.

### 83.

1 ... Ba4 wins the exchange.

### 84.

Leave the bishop sit on f6 in favor of 1 ... Qxc3+ 2 Qd2 Qxa1+ followed by trading queens and then ... gxf6, emerging a rook ahead.

### 85.

1 ... d2 2 Bxd2 Bd3 and the upcoming discovered check wins at least the queen for a rook.

### 86.

1 ... Ne5, forces the queen away from the c3-knight. (a) 2 Qxd4 (or Qd2) 2 ... Nxf3+, (b) 2 Qe3 Nc2+.

## 87.

1 ... Rxh2+ 2 Kg1 Qxe2, striking through the body of the g2-rook. Also 2 ... Rah8 is strong.

## 88.

1 ... Rxd1+ 2 Bxd1 Re1+ and 3 ... Rxd1.

## 89.

1 Nxe7+ Nxe7 2 Bxb7.

## 90.

1 Qg7 picks up the f8-rook.

## 91.

1 ... d1/Q+ is good enough. Also 1 ... Rxd4 2 Qxd4 Rd8 with promotion shortly. In any case Black wins at least a rook for the d-pawn.

## 92.

1 Be5 Qd7 (Black's queen must stay on the d-file to prevent 2 Bd6+, winning the knight on e8) 2 Qb4+ Qe7 3 Qxa5.

## 93.

Black could take the bishop (1 ... Nxd8) but there's more to be had. 1 ... Rf2+ (a) 2 Kg1 Rxa2+ (b) 2 Ke1 Rxg2 with 3 ... Rg1+, and 3 ... Nxd8 on tap.

## 94.

1 ... Nxc3 2 Qc2 cxd4 supports the knight and gains two pawns.

## 95.

1 h7+ Kxh7 (if 1 ... Qxh7 2 Nh6+ and 1 ... Bxh7 2 Nh6#) 2 g6+ Kxg6 3 Ne5+. Or 2 ... Bxg6 3 Qh3+ Kg8 4 Nh6+.

## 96.

1 e5 Nh5 2 g4 snares the knight. Exchanging 1 ... dxe5 2 dxe5 Bxf3 3 Bxf3 Nh5 doesn't help Black's cause. Apart from g4, White also has 4 Bxa8 and 4 Bc6.

## 97.

1 ... Bc5 2 Bg3 Bd4 forks b2 and e5. If 2 f3 then 2 ... Nf2 3 Rg1 Nd3+ wins the exchange.

## 98.

1 … Rxd5 2 exd5 Bxc4 and 3 … Bxa2 or Bxf1.

## 99.

1 … Qxd4? 2 Bb2 with 3 Qxc8+ in reserve. So, Black should retreat 1 … Qd8.

## 100.

1 Qf5+ is clever; 1 … Nxf5? 2 exf5#. But best is 1 Rxg7+ Kxg7 2 Qh3 and there's nothing to be done against 4 Qh7(+) followed by taking the knight.

## 100A.

1 Bxc4 dxc4 2 Qxc4+ and 3 Qxc6.

## 100B.

1 Rb1 threatening 2 Nxd4 Qxd4? 3 Be3. Black can't avoid loss of the bishop.

## 101.

1 … Qxa2+ 2 Kxa2 Ra5+ 3 Kb2 Ba3+ 4 Ka1 Bc1#.

## 102.

1 Be3! along with 2 c3 Nc6 3 bxc5 picks off a pawn. Less convincing is the immediate 1 c3 Nc6 2 bxc5 dxc5 3 Qxc5 Nd4.

## 103.

1 Rxe7 Qxf7 (1 … Qxe7 2 Qxg8+) 2 Rxf7 Be7 3 c6 and 4 Rxd7(+).

## 104.

1 Rh7+ Kxh7 2 Nxf6+ Kg7 3 Nxd7.

## 105.

1 Rxf5 Bxf5 2 Nxd6+ Kb8 3 Nxf5+.

## 106.

1 h3 Bh5 2 Rg1 g5 (else the bishop gets trapped by g2-g4) 3 fxg5 gains White a pawn.

## 107.

1 … Bh6 2 Qxh6 Qxf2+, forcing mate in two.

## 108.

1 Rh3 threatens 2 hxg5 fxg5 3 f6 busting in. The best Black can do is drop a pawn after 1 … g4 2 Rg3 and 3 Rxg4.

## 109.
If 1 Qb7+ Bc7, so 1 Bxc5 Bxc5 2 Qb7+ Kd8 (2 … Kd6 3 Qe7#) 3 Qxa8+ etc.

## 110.
1 Rxa7 Kxa7 2 Kd2 and nothing can prevent 3 Ra1+ followed by mate.

## 111.
1 Qh8+ Kxg5 2 Nf3+ Kf4 3 Qh6+ g5 4 Qxg5#.

## 112.
1 exd5 exd5 2 Nxd5 wins a pawn: if 2 … Qxd5? 3 Bxh7+ and 4 Rxd5.

## 113.
1 Nf6 Qxf6 2 Qxe8+ Kg7 3 Re7+ etc.

## 114.
1 Qe7 (if 1 … Rxe7 2 Rf8#) 1 … Qc7 2 Qf8+ Rxf8 3 Rxf8#.

## 115.
1 Qxc6+ bxc6 2 Rb8+ Kd7 3 R1b7#.

## 116.
1 … Qf2+, wins the d4-rook, for if 2 Kxf2 Bd4+ 3. Kg3 (3 Ke2 Rf2#) 3 … Bf2#!

## 117.
1 … Rxb2 2 Rxb2 Qxc5+, with a winning endgame. If 2 Qxe3 Rb1# or 2 Kxb2 Qb3+ 3 Kc1 (or a1) Qb1#. A trap prepared for Kasparov by X3D Fritz during their match in November 2003, which Gary did not fall into!

## 118.
1 g4 N-moves 2 g5 Q-moves 3 Qxd4+.

## 119.
1 Nxf7 Kxf7 2 Bxc6 Bxc6 3 Qxc6 Qxc6 4 Ne5+ and 5 Nxc6.

## 120.
1 … Qc2 (threatens mate by 2 … Rd1) 2 Be2 Qc1+ 3 Kf2 Qxh1, and Black is the exchange up.

## 121.
1 … Nxb3 gains a pawn as 2 Qxb3? Rd1+ 3 Ka2 Bd5 drops the queen.

## 122.

1 Kb1 Qxd1+ 2 Nxd1 Rxa2 3 c7 and promotes. There may (or may not) be other ways but this is certainly the cleanest.

## 123.

1 Qf8+ Rxf8 2 Rxf8+ Kxf8 3 Nxd7+, followed by 4 Nxd5 winning a piece.

## 124.

1 Bf4 Qf2 (or 1 ... Qh4) 2 Nb6+ axb6 3 Qxc6+ bxc6 4 Ba6#.

## 125.

1 Bxc6 dxc6 2 Qh8+ Qf8 3 Qe5+ and 4 Qxb8.

## 126.

1 ... Bxh2+ 2 Kxh2 Qh4+ 3 Kg1 Qf2+, and keeps on checking. Black is behind and correctly makes for the draw.

## 127.

1 ... Qb4+ 2 Bxb4 a(c)xb4+ 3 Ka4 Ra1 forces a quick mate (if 4 Qxa1 b5#).

## 128.

1 ... Nxd5 2 exd5 (2 Bxe7 Ndxe7) 2 ... Bxg5 3 dxc6 bxc6 wins a pawn for Black.

## 129.

1 ... Nxd4+ 2 exd4 Qf3+ 3 Ke1 Nd3+ 4 Qxd3 exd3 and 5 ... Qe2#.

## 130.

1 ... Qxc5 2 dxc5 Rxd1+ 3 Kh2 Rxb1 with two rooks and a bishop for the queen.

## 131.

1 Rxg7+ Kxg7 2 Qg6+ Kh8 3 Qh7#.

## 132.

Black gets control of e4 by 1 ... Bxd2+ 2 Qxd2 Qc6 3 Qh2 and now 4 ... Qe4+.

## 133.

1 Nc5 Bc8 2 Nxa6 bxa6 3 Bxc6.

## 134.

1 gxf6+ (a) 1 ... Kxf6 2 Qg7+ Ke7 3 Bg5+ Ke8 4 Rxh8+ Nxh8 5 Qg8# (b) 1 ... Ke8 2 Rg8+ Rxg8 3 Qxg8#.

## 135.
1 Rxg7+ Rxg7 2 Qxh6+ Kg8 3 Qxg7#.

## 136.
1 hxg5 fxg5 2 Nxg5 Bxg5 3 Bxg5 Qxg5 4 Qxg5 hxg5 5 Kg3+ recovers the piece and wins a pawn. (a) 5 … Nh6 6 Rxh6+ Kg8 7 Rxd6 (b) 5 … Nh5 6 Rxh5+ Kg7 7 Rxg5+.

## 137.
1 … Qd4+ 2 Kh1 Qd1+ 3 Rxd1 Rd1#.

## 138.
1 Bxf7+ Kg7 2 Bg8+ Kf6 (or 2 … Kh8 3 Rxh7#) 3. Rf7#.

## 139.
1 hxg6 hxg5 2 Nh6+ gxh6 3 g7 decides.

## 140.
1 … Nexf2 2 Nxf2 Nxe3 3 Q-moves Nxg2+.

## 141.
1 Qf5+ g6 (1 … Kh8 2 Qc8+ and 3 Qg8#) 2 Qd7 with the threat of 3 Kf6(f8)+ and 4 Qg7#.

## 142.
1 Nxd5 Nxd5 2 Qh8+ Bxh8 3 Rxh8#.

## 143.
1 f4+ Kf5 (1 … Kh5 2 Rxh6+ Kxh6 3 Qxg4) 2 Rf6+ Kxf6 3 Qxg4 with a winning endgame.

## 144.
1 … Rb8 2 Qa6 Nb4 3 Qxa7 Ra6 catches the queen.

## 145.
1 f4 Bxf4+ 2 Rxf4+ exf4+ 3 Kxd2.

## 146.
1 … Rxf3, and if 2 Bxf3 Qxh2+ 3 Kf1 Qxf2#.

## 147.
1 Nf7+ Qxf7 2 Qh4+ Kg8 3 Qxd8. The knight fork sets up the queen fork. Or one good fork deserves another.

## 148.
1 … Rc1+ 2 Rxc1 Rxc1+ 3 Qf1 Rxf1+ 4 Kxf1 Qxb5+.

### 149.
1 Ng5 Rxf2 2 Qxh7+ Kf8 3 Qh8#. If 1 … Nxf6 2 Rxf6 and Black still loses.

### 150.
1 … Qh4+ 2 Kf1 Re1+ 3 Rxe1 Q(R)xe1#.

### 151.
1 … Nxe4 (a) 2 Qxd8 Nxf2+ 3 Rxf2 Rxd8, (b) 2 Nxe4 (or dxe4) … Qxh4 3 Nxh4 Bxh6, (c) 2 Bg5 Nxf2+ etc.

### 152.
1 … Ra3+ (if 1 … Qa7 2 Qxc8+ and Black gets mated!) wins White's queen, for if 2 Kxa3 Qa7+ is mate in two.

### 153.
1 Nxd4 cxd4 (1 … Qxd4 2 c3) 2 Qxb4 dxe3 3 Bxe3 wins a pawn.

### 154.
1 Rf1+ Nf3 (1 … Kg7 2 Qh7#) 2 Rxf3+ Ke5 3 Qg3+ Kd4 4 Nxe6#.

### 155.
1 gxf6 Rf8 2 f7+ Kh8 (2 … Rxf7 3 Nh6+) 3 Ke7 Ra8 4 f8/Q+.

### 156.
1 Bf6 gxf6 2 exf6 Rg8 3 Rd8 mates in two.

### 157.
1 Qh6+ Kf7 2 Bf3 Qf4 (2 … Qxc4 3 Kxg3) 3 Qh3 and the bishop has no escape.

### 158.
1 Ne5 menaces mate forcing the win of material: (a) 1 … Nxe5 2 Qxe5+ and 3 Qxh8, (b) 1 … Qe7 2 Nxc6 and if 2 … dxc6 3 Qxc6+ with 4 Qxa8+.

### 159.
1 … Rxf2 (a) 2 Bxg5 Rxf1# (b) 2 Rxf2 Rxf2 3 Bxg5 (3 Qxf2 Bxf2 check!) 3 … Rxc2+ and Black emerges on top.

### 160.
1 Bxh3 Qxh3 2 Qxe3 Qg2 3 0-0-0 with an extra piece.

### 161.
1 Nc6+ Nxc6 2 Ra4+ Na5 3 Rxa5#.

### 162.
When behind, don't fool around. Just make a draw: 1 Nf6+ Kh6 2 Ng4+ Kh7 3 Nf6+ with perpetual check.

## 163.

1 … Bd8 2 Ne3 (avoiding … c6) 2 … Bxh3 3 Nxh3 Ng5 smashing in on the h-file.

## 164.

1 Nxf7 Kxf7 2 Qxh7+ Kf8 3 Re7 with mate coming up. There's also 1 Nxh7 Nxh7 2 Rh5 gxh5 3 Qxb6.

## 165.

1 b4 axb4 2 axb4 Rc1 3 Bxb5 wins a pawn.

## 166.

1 Nxb7 gathers up the exchange, for if 1 … Bxb7 2 Nxe6+ wins the queen.

## 167.

1 … Bh6 2 Re1 Bxe4 3 (R)xe4 Qxg3.

## 168.

1 … Bxb5 2 Rc8+ Ke7 3 Rxh8 Bxe2 with material advantage of two bishops for a rook.

## 169.

1 Rc7 Qf8 (1 … Rd7 2 Rxd7 Qxd7 3 Rxd6) 2 Rxd6 Rxd6 3 Qxb7 with two minors for the rook.

## 170.

1 … Nb8, in conjunction with 2 … Nxa6. 2 Bc8 is insufficient in view of 2 … Qxc8 3 Qxf6 Bxb5, but it's a bit sticky.

## 171.

1 g3 stops 2 … Qxh2+ 3 Kf1 Qh1# and threatens 2 Nxf7 Qxf7 3 Re7. There's no defense. If 1 … Rd7 2 Ne6+ and 1 … Nh6 2 Nxf7 Nxf7 still loses to 3 Re7.

## 172.

1 Qb3 Nd5 (1 … Ng4 2 Re8#) 2 Rf3 Qd6 3 Re8+ crush.

## 173.

1 … Qxa2 2 Rxc3 (2 Ra1 Qc4) 2 … Rxc3, and Black keeps his three extra pawns since 3 Bxc3? fails to 3 … Qxe2.

## 174.

1 d8/Q+ Qxd8 2 Qb3+ Kg7 3 Qxa3.

## 175.

1 Qe8+ Bf8 2 Qxf7+ Kh8 3 Qxh7# (Qxf8#).

## 176.

1 Rg8+ Kh7 2 Qg6+ fxg6 3 fxg6+ Kxg8 4 f7#.

## 177.

1 Rc6+ Kd7 2 Nc2 Rd2 3 Kxa4.

## 178.

1 ... Kc6 2 Nb8+ Kb7 3 Nd7 Kc7 wins the knight.

## 179.

1 Rxf6 Nxf6 2 Rxf6 Kxf6 3 Nh5+ gxh5 4 Qxh6#.

## 180.

1 Qxa7+ Nxa7 2 Nb6+ Kb8 3 Nxd7+ Kc7 4 Nxf6 with a winning endgame.

## 181.

1 ... Nxb4 2 Qc7 Qxc7 3 Nxc7 a5, and Black is for choice.

## 182.

1 ... Bxf2+ (a) 2 Kxf2 e3+ 3 Kxe3 Rfe8+ leads to mate and (b) 2 Kh1 Nd4, with multiple threats: 3 ... e3# 3 ... Qxb7 3 ... Bxe1.

## 183.

1 Ned6+ Bxd6 2 Nxd6+ Kd8 3 Nxe8 wins the exchange.

## 184.

1 ... Qd2? 2 Nf2 holds. 1 ... Qh2, (a) 2 Ng5 Qd2, (b) 2 Nf2 Qh5+ 3 Kg2 Qe2.

## 185.

If 1 ... Bxb4 2 Rc8+ gives annoying counterplay. So cleanest is 1 ... Rh5 2 Rh1 (else 2 ... Rh2#) 2 ... Rxh1 3 Rxh1 and now 3 ... Bxb4.

## 186.

1 Kg2 threatening 2 f3 pushes the queen away, 1 ... Qd1, after which White pursues the king 2 Bxh6 Bc3 3 Qxf5+ and White is three pawns up.

## 187.

1 Bxh6 gxh6 2 Qxh6 threatening 3 Nf6#. Black will have to give up the queen to stop mate. Note 2 ... Ng6 3 Qxg6+.

## 188.

1 ... Rxb2 2 Nc5 Bb6, and the knight is lost. E.g. 3 Kd4 Kd6, or 3 ... Rd2+ 4 Ke3 Rd8 etc.

## 189.

1 ... Qa2+ 2 Nxa2 (2 Kc3 Qb2#) Rgxa2 and nothing can prevent 3 ... R8a3#.

## 190.
1 ... Qxf2+ 2 Kxf2 Bc5+ 3 Rd4 Bxd4#.

## 191.
1 Qxd7 Qxd7 2 Rb8+ Kf7 3 Ne5+ and 4 Nxd7.

## 192.
1 axb6 Qxb3 2 bxa7 Qxb2 3 a8/Q Qxc3 4 Qxe8+ Kh7 5 Qxf7 and White, exercising care, will win this endgame with his extra bishop.

## 193.
1 Rxd6+ Qxd6 2 Qxd8+ Kxd8 3 Nxf7+ and 4 Nxd6. 1 Qxd8+ also works. In any case White has two extra pawns for the ending.

## 194.
1 f3 Nf6 2 Nc5 Qxb4 3 Na6 and 4 Nxb8 or Nxc7.

## 195.
1 Qf4+ Kg7 2 Qf6+ Kg8 3 Rh2 and 4 Rh8#.

## 196.
1 ... Bb4+ 2 c3 Bxc3+ 3 bxc3 Qxc3+ and 4 ... Qxa1+. If 2 Bd2 Qxd2+ 3 Qxd2 Bxd2+ 4 Kxd2 exf4.

## 197.
1 ... Rxg3 2 Rxg3 Bxf4+ 3 Kb1 Bxg3.

## 198.
1 Nf6+ gxf6 2 Bxf6+ Ng7 3 Qxg7#.

## 199.
1 Ne6 (if 1 ... fxe6 2 Bxg6 with a quick mate) 1 ... Nxe6 2 Qh7+ Kf8 3 Rxf7 Kxf7 4 Rf3+ and mate next move.

## 200.
1 Rxf6 exf6 2 Rxf6 Rxf6 (2 ... Qxb3 3 Rf8#) 3 Bxf6+ Kg8 4 Bxd8 wins a piece; the queen is pinned.

## 200A.
1 Rxf6 (a) 1 ... Rxf6 2 Qh7 with 3 Qh8 (g8)+ (b) 1 ... gxf6 2 Qxh6+ Kg8 (3 ... Rg7 4 Qh8+) 3 Re3 and then 4 Rg3+decides.

## 200B.
Black forces off the queens by 1 ... Qf3+ 2 Ke5 Qf6+ 3 Kd5 Qd6+ 4 Kc4(e4) Qe6+. After that it's an easy win.

## 201.
1 Rxh6+ Kxh6 2 Qf6+ Kh7 3 Rh1+ Kg8 4 Rh8#.

## 202.
1 Rxe6+ (a) 1 … fxe6 2 Qxf8# (b) 1 … Re7 2 Qxf7+ (c) 1 … Kd8 2 Qxf8+ Kc7 3 Qc5+ Kd8 4 Rh6 etc.

## 203.
1 … Kf6 2 Ng8+ Kg7 3 Ne7 Kf7 4 Nf5 Be4+, winning the knight, for if 5 Kxe4 c2, and the pawn queens.

## 204.
1 Qxf8+ Qxf8 2 Nb5 Qc5 3 Nd6+ Kd8 4 c7+ Qxc7 5 Rxc7 Kxc7 6 h6 etc.

## 205.
1 … Bh6 2 Rc2 Re3 3 Bf3 Rxc3 4 Rxc3 Qxc3 winning a piece, for if 5 Bd5+ Nxd5 protects Black's queen.

## 206.
1 … Qa1+ 2 Kg2 f3+ 3 Kh2 Qxh1+ 4 Kxh1 f2 and promotes, unless White cedes the queen.

## 207.
1 Rxg7+ (a) 1 … Bxg7 2 Ng5+ and 3 Nxf3 (b) 1 … Ke8 2 Nxc7+ Kf8 3 Ne6+ Ke8 4 Rh7.

## 208.
1 … Qg6 along with 2 … Bxh3 and 3 … Rh5. If 2 Rf6 then 2 … Rg2+ 3 Kh1 Rh2+ and mate next at g2.

## 209.
1 Rxc8 Rxc8 2 Qxc8+ Bxc8 3 Rxc8+ Kg7 4 Bxa6 gives White rook and two minors for the queen.

## 210.
Push the king away, 1 Re7+ Kd8 2 Nf7+ Kc8 3 Re8+ Kb7, then take the knight 4 Rxf8.

## 211.
1 Nf6+ (a) 1 … Bxf6 2 Qh7+ Kf8 3 Qxf7# (b) 1 … Kf8 2 Nd7+ Bxd7 3 Rxf7+ Kg8 4 Qh7#.

## 212.
1 Qe8+ Qf8 2 Qe6+ Kh8 3 Qe5+ Kg8 4 Qxb2.

## 213.

1 Nb3 Qc6 2 Nxc4 Qxc4 3 Qxc4 dxc4 4 Rxd8+ wins: 4 ... Ke7 5 Rxc8 cxb3 6 Rc7+ Kd8 7 Rc4 bxa2 (7 ... b5 8 Rd4+) 8 Ra4 etc.

## 214.

1 ... Qxd4 wins a piece, for if 2 Bxg5+ hxg5 3 Qxd4 Nf3+ 4 gxf3 Bxd4.

## 215.

1 Bf3 Bb7 2 Be4 is zugswang No. 1 and 2 ... Ba8 3 b5 axb5 4 a6 is zugswang No. 2. Black must let the White king in. E.g. 4 ... b4 5 Bc2 Ke8 6 Kf6 Kd7 7 Kf7 etc.

## 216.

The knight can safely be taken 1. dxe5, as 1 ... d4 is met by 2 Nf3 g6 (2 ... dxe3 3 Bxh7+ and 4 Rxd8) 3 Bb5 and White picks off the d-pawn.

## 217.

1 ... Bh6 2 Re2 Rd2 3 Rxd2 Rxd2. The rook attacks c2 and g2 forcing White to give up the queen, 4 Qxd2 Bxd2. The e4-knight was neutralized by the diagonal pin, g6-c2.

## 218.

1 Bxh4 Bxh4 2 Qxd7 Qxd7 3 Rxh4+ Qh7 4 Rxh7+ gains a pawn.

## 219.

1 Rfe1 Qd7 2 Rxe7 Qxe7 3 Bxd6 Q-moves 4 Bxf8.

## 220.

1 Na4 Qb4 2 a3 Qb5 3 Rxc6 bxc6 4 Qxd4.

## 221.

1 Nxf6+ gxf6 2 Kb1 Kg7 (if 2 ... Qa3 3 Bc1 Qc5 4 Bh6 wins) 3 Qg4+ Kh8 4 Qf5 Kg7 5 Bh6+ mates in two.

## 222.

1 ... f3+ (a) 2 Kxf3 Rf1+ and 3 ... a1/Q (b) 2 Kh2 f2 (c) 2 Kf2 Rh1 3 Rxa2 Rh2+ 4 Kxf3 Rxa2.

## 223.

1 Qxc8 Rxc8 2 Rxd4 and White emerges with two pieces for a rook after say 2 ... Be5 3 Bxe3 Bxd4 4 Bxd4.

## 224.

1 Rc5 (a) 1 ... Qe1 2 Rh5+ gxh5 3 Qf6# (b) 1 ... Rb5 2 Qe3+ Kg7 3 Qe5+ f6 4 Rxb5.

## 225.

1 Rb7 threatens Rxb6 forcing 1 … Rxb5. But on the 5th rank the rook has no effective check and White has time to promote the h-pawn: 2 Kg6 Kf8 3 h6 with 4 Rb8+ 5. h7 etc.

## 226.

1 Rab1 Qd3 2 Qxf8+ Kxf8 3 Rb8+ Ke7 4 Rc7#.

## 227.

1 Nc6 (a) 1 … Qe6 2 Nxd8 (b) 1 … Qd6 2 Rxd5 Qxd5 3 Nxd8. (c) 1 … Bxb3 2 Rxd8+ Kf7 3 Bxb3+ Kf6 4 Nxe5.

## 228.

1 Qg4 (a) 1 … Rdc7 (or 1 … Nb8) 2 Bxg7 (b) 1 … Rcc7 2 Re8+ Kf7 3 Qxg7+ Kxe8 4 Qg8#.

## 229.

1 Nxc5 Bxg5 2 Qa4+ Kf8 3 Nxg5 Qxg5 4 Qc6 infiltrates and wins. If 4 … Rb8 5 Qd6+.

## 230.

1 Rg7 Nh6 2 Rh7 Ng8 3 Rh8 Rg4 4 f7.

## 231.

1 Qf4+ Kg8 2 Qf7+ Kh8 3 Rxd6 (a) 3 … Rxd6 4 Qf8# (b) 3 … Rg8 4 Qxg8+ Kxg8 5 Rd8# (c) other third moves also leave White ahead.

## 232.

1 … Bb4+ 2 Ke2 Ba6+ 3 Kf3 Qxd5+ 4 Rxd5 Bxf1.

## 233.

1 Bd3 Ng7 2 Bg6 Qd8 (2 … Qe7 3 Rc6) 3 Bh7+ Kh8 4 Qg6 and White has broken into Black's camp. The main threat is 5 Qxh6 along with 6 Bg6+ and 7 Qh7#.

## 234.

1 Nh6+ Kh8 2 Qf7 Nf6 3 Qg8+ Nxg8 4 Nf7#.

## 235.

1 Bxf7+ Kxf7 (1 … Kh8 lasts longer but leads to a lost endgame after 2 Qxh5 gxh5 3 Bxh5) 2 Rxd7+ Bxd7 3 Rxd7+ Ke8 4 Qg7 forces mate.

## 236.

1 … Bxf3 2 Kg1 Bxe2 wins the exchange. If 2 gxf3 Rxf3+ yields a mating attack: (a) 3 Ke1 Rxf1+ 4 Kxf1 Qg1# (b) 3 Kxf3 Rf7+ 4 Bf6 Rxf6+ 5 Rf5 Rxf5+ 6 Ke4 Qe6(g4)#.

## 237.

1 Nxf8 (threat 2 Qd7+ Kxf8 3 Na4+) 1 … Rxc5 2 Qd7+ Kxf8 3 Bxc5+ Qxc5 4 Qd8#.

## 238.

1 f6+ Ke8 2 f7+ Ke7 3 Rxd8 Kxd8 4 f8/Q+.

## 239.

1 Rd6 (a) 1 … Qxd6 or 1 … Bf7 2 Qg7# (b) 1 … Bc8 2 c5+ (c) 1 … Re8 2 Rxe6 Rxe6 3 c5 Nf8 4 Bxe6+ winning a piece.

## 240.

1 … Rg4 mates or wins the queen. (a) 2 Rf2 Rh4+ (but not 2 … Qxf2? 3 Qe8+ etc.) (b) 2 Rg2 Qxf3+ 3 Rg3 Rxg3+ (also 3 … Qf1+) 4 hxg3 Qh1#.

## 241.

1 Rxc7 Kxc7 2 Bxe5+ Kb6 3 Bxg7 Rg8 4 Rxf7 with three pawns for the exchange.

## 242.

1 Qc4 Ke6 2 Qg4+ Kf7 3 Qxd7+ Nxd7 4 Nxd5 leaves White a piece up.

## 243.

1 … Qxc5 2 Nxc5 Bxg2. The threat 3 … Bf3#, forces White to return the queen: 3 Qh5 Bd5+ 4 Qxg6 hxg6, and Black emerges with an extra pawn.

## 244.

1 … Bxf5 2 exf5 Rxg2 breaking in: (a) 3 Kxg2 Ne3+ (b) 3 Bg3 Rxg3 4 hxg3 Nf2+ (c) 3 d4 Rxh2+ 4 Kg1 Qa8 etc. (d) 3 Rc8+ Kh7 4 d4 Rxh2+ 5 Kg1 Bxd4+.

## 245.

1 hxg6? Qf2+ 2 Kh1 hxg6 3 Qxg6+ Kh8 threatening 4 … Rh7+ is dangerous only for White. The safe way is 1 Qg2 Rg7 2 h6 Rf7 3 Rxe5 and d5 falls shortly.

## 246.

Not 1 Kxg2? Qc6+. But 1 Kg1 wins quickly enough. E.g. 1 … Qc6 2 Rf6+ Kg5 3 Rg7+ Kh4 4 Rf3#.

## 247.

1 a3 Na6(Nc6) 2 Nd5 (a) 2 ...
Qd8 3 Bxf6 gxf6 4 Qh5# (b) 2
... Qf7 3 Nxf6+ and 4 Bxf7
(c) 2 ... Qe4 3 f3 Qe5 4 Bf4
traps the queen.

## 248.

1 Qa2 Nf8 2 Nc5 wins the
e6-pawn. If 2 ... g6 3 Bxg6
Nxg6 4 Qxe6+ and 5 Qxc8.

## 249.

1 Rb5 Qd8 2 Rxb8+ Qxb8 3
Qf5 (threat Rc8+) 3 ... g6 (3
... Rb1+ 4 Kh2 e4+ 5 g3
changes nothing) 4 Rc8+ Kg7,
Qxf6+ and 6 Rxb8.

## 250.

1 ... Nxe4 2 Qd1 (2 dxe4
Nxf3+ 3 Bxf3 Qxd2 4 Bxd2
Rxd2 is also a lost ending) 2
... Nxf3+ 3 B(R)xf3 Nxg5
wins a piece.

## 251.

1 Rxe7 Nxe7 2 Nf6+ Kg7 3
Nd5+ f6 4 Nxe7 Re8 5 Rf1
etc.

## 252.

1 ... Nxe7? lets the queen
escape 2 Qxf6. So, 1 ... c3 (a)
2 Bxc3 Bxc3 3 Rxc3 Nxe7 (b)
2 Ba3 Nxe7 (not 2 ... Nh6 3
Qf8 and things are still messy)
3 Qxe8+ Bxe8 4 Rxe7 Bc6
and Black should win by
virtue of his larger force.

## 253.

Best to take the knight
removing an attacker, and
then run with the king: 1 ...
gxh6 2 Qg6+ Kf8 3 Qxh6+
Ke8 4 Bg6+ Kd8 5 Qxg5+
Kc7 and Black is safe, for if 6
Qxf4 Qxg1+. In the game.
Black allowed himself to be
bluffed and played 1 ... Kf8.

## 254.

1 Nxe5 Rxe5 2 Bf4 Re8 3 e5
Bxg2 (if N-moves, 4 Bxb7) 4
exf6 and both Black bishops
are en prise.

## 255.

1 Qxh6+ Kxh6 2 Nf5+ Kh7 (2
... Kh5 3 Nf4#) 3 Rh3+ Kg6
4 Rh6#.

## 256.

1 ... Nxh2 2 Kxh2 Ng4+ 3 fxg4 Qh4+ 4 Kg1 Bxg3 and mate shortly.

## 257.

1 Bxf5 Bxf5 (1 ... Rg7 2 Bxh7) 2 Qf6+ Rg7 3 Nxf5 Qf8 4 d6 and wins. White exchanges twice on g7 then promotes the d-pawn.

## 258.

1 Bxf7+ clips a pawn, for if 1 ... Rxf7 2 Qd8+ Kg7 3 Rxf7+ Kxf7 4 Rf1+ Bf5 5 Qxa8 gaining the exchange. Therefore 1 ... Kh8 is forced with a technically lost position.

## 259.

1 Rxg6+ Rg7, so 1 Qxg6+ Kf8 (now on 1 ... Rg7 2 Qe8#) 2 Rh8+ Ke7 3 Qxf7+ Kxf7 4 Rh7+ and 5 Rxc7.

## 260.

1 g4 opens the sluice gates. 1 ... fxg4 2 Be4 Rg7 3 f5 gxf5 4 Bxf5+ Kh8 5 Qxh6+ Kg8 6 Be6+ etc.

## 261.

1 Qe6+ Kh8 (1 ... Kg7 2 Rf7+ Kh6 3 Rxh7+) 2 Nxg6+ hxg6 3 Qxg6 Nf6 4 Rxf6 and 5 Qh7#.

## 262.

1 Qxh6+ gxh6 (1 ... Kg8 2 Bxf6) 2 Bxf6+ Bg7 3 Bxg7+ Kg8 4 Bf6+ Kf8 5 Bh7 and Rg8#.

## 263.

1 Nxb7 Kxb7 2 Rc7+ and 3 Rxe7 gets things rolling. But you also have to examine 1 ... Bxc2 2 Nxd6 Bxb3 3 Nf7 Rf8 4 axb3 Rxf7 and now 5 Rc5 is very much in White's favor. Apart from taking the d-pawn (Bxd5), there's also the maneuver 6 Rb5+ and 7 Rb7 placing Black in a bind.

## 264.

1 ... Ne4 (a) 2 Bxg7 Qh4+ 3 Kd1 (3 g3 Nxg3) 3 ... Nf2+ 4 Ke1 Nd3+ 5 Kd1 Qe1+ 6 Rxe1 Nf2# (b) 2 Qb2 Qh4+ 3 g3 Nxg3 4 Bxg3 Qxg3+ and 5 ... Bxb2 (c) 2 d4 Bxe5 3 dxe5 Qh4+ 4 Kd1 Rd8+ 5 Bd3 Bg4#.

## 265.

1 Rxe5+ (a) 1 ... Re6 2 Rxe6+ fxe6 3 Qxe6+ Kf8 4 Nd7+ (b) 1 ... Kf8 2 Re7 Rf6 (2 ... f6 3 Qe6) 3 Nd7+ (c) 1 ... Bxe5 2 Qxe5+ Kf8 (2 ... Re6 3 Qh8#) 3 d7 readying 4 Qxb8 Qxb8 5 d8/Q+.

## 266.

Black stays afloat with 1 ... Bxd4 (a) 2 cxd4 Rd5 3 Bxf6 gxf6 4 exf6 Rf5 and 5 ... Rxf6 (b) 2 Rxd4 Rxd4 3 Rxd4 Nd7.

## 267.

1 Kh4 and Black is stuck for moves. (a) 1 ... Rf7 2 Kh5 and 3 Rxh6# (b) 1 ... Re4 2 Rg7+ Kh8 3 Re7+ (c) 1 ... Rd7 2 g5 hxg5 3 Kxg5 Bf7 4 Rh6+ Kg8 5 Rh8#.

## 268.

1 Nxc5 Rxc5 (1 ... Bxc5 2 Qxg7) 2 Ba4+ Ke7 3 Bg5+ f6 4 exf6+ gxf6 5 Nxe6.

## 269.

Not 1 g4 Kh8 2 gxf5 Rxf5 with equality but 1 Qe5 Qxe5 (1 ... b6 2 Qxa5 bxa5 3 g4) 2 dxe5 Ne3 3 Rxd6 Rxd6 4 exd6 Nxf1 5 d7 and promotes.

## 270.

1 Qh8+ Ke7 2 Rxf7+ Kd8 3 Rxd7+ Kxd7 4 Qxe8+ Kxe8 5 Bf7+ Kxf7 6 Rxb4.

## 271.

1 Qc5 (not 1 e4? Qb6+) 1 ... Be6 (1 ... Qf6 2 Bg5; 1 ... Nce7, e4 Qb6 3 Bd6) 2 e4 Nc3 3 Rxd8 Nxe4+ 4 Kg1 Nxc5 5 Rxf8+ Rxf8 6 Bd6 gains the exchange.

## 272.

1 ... Nxd5 (a) 2 Bxe7 Nxe7 (also 2 ... Bxa6) 3 Bxb7 Qxb7 4 Qxd7 Qxg2 5 Qxe7 Qxh1 (b) 2 Bxb7 Qxb7 3 Bxe7 (3 Qxd7 Bxg5) 3 ... b5 4 Qa3 b4 5 Qa4 N7b6 and 6 ... Nxe7 wins a piece.

## 273.

1 Rxc8+ Kf7 2 Qe8+ (2 Qf3+ also works) 2 ... Kf6 3 Qe5+ Kf7 4 Qf5+ Ke7 5 Rc7+ and 6 Qc8#.

## 274.

1 Nxe4 dxe4 2 Qc4+ Kh8 3 Nf7+ Rxf7 (3 ... Kg8 4 Nh6+ Kg8 5 Qg8+ with smothered mate) 4 Qxf7 and White is winning. If 4 ... exd3 5 Re8+ etc.

## 275.

1 ... Rfc8 2 Bc4 Rxc4 3 Qxc4 Qa1+ 4 Kc2 Qxb2+ 5 Kd3 Ra3+ and mate next.

## 276.

1 Be5 Rxf1+ 2 Rxf1 (a )2 ... Qxh4 (or 2 ... hxg5) 3 Rf8# (b) 2 ... Bxe5 3 Qxh6 and mate at f8 or f7 (c) 2 ... Qxe5 3 Nf7+ Kxh7 4 Nxe5 Bxe5 5 Qe7+ etc.

## 277.

1 fxg6 hxg6 2 Qh8+ Kf7 3 Rh7+ Nxh7 4 Qxh7+ Kf8 5 Qxg6 and White has a winning attack. The threat is 6 Rxf6+.

## 278.

1 Nxd5 Qxd5 (1 ... R(N)xd5 2 Bxc4 bxc4 3 Rxc4+) 2 Rxc4 bxc4 3 Bxc4 Qb7 4 Be6+ fxe6 5 Rc1+.

## 279.

Although 1 ... f6 should win in the long run, 1 ... Nd4 is certainly the most elegant solution. If 2. Nxd4 Qxh1# or 2 Bxd4 Qc1#, and if 2 Qxd4 Qc2+ and mate in two.

## 280.

1 Ng6+ Kh7 2 Nxe7 Qxe7 3 Qxe7 Bxe7 4 Rfe1 Bc8 5 d5 emerging the exchange ahead.

## 281.

1 Qxg6 hxg6 2 Bxf7+ Rxf7 3 Rh8+ Kxh8 4 Nxf7+ and 5 Nxd6.

## 282.

1 Rxc5 Qxc5 2 Qxc5 Rxc5 3 b7 Rc1 4 b8/Q Bh3 5 Rb1 and wins.

## 283.

1 ... Qxh3 2 Rxe1 Qxg3+ 3 Kf1 Ng4 4 Re2 Ne3+ 5 Rxe3 dxe3 and wins.

## 284.

1 Ra1 Qxb2 (1 ... Qd5 2 Be4) 2 Re2 Qc3 3 Rc2 Qxd4 4 Bb5+ axb5 5 Qxd4 Rxa1+ 6 Qxa1 and White is up a queen for two minor pieces and two weak pawns.

## 285.

1 ... a4 2 Qc4 (if 2 Qc3 e4 wins a piece) b5 3 Qxb5 Ba6 4 Qxa4 Bxd3.

## 286.

1 Bg5 Bc7 (1 ... fxg5 2 g7 and Black cannot prevent 3 Bh7+) 2 Bxf6 e4 3 Bxe4 Bf4+ 4 Kh5 Be6 (forced) 5 Bd5 and the passed pawns win easily.

## 287.

1 Nxe6 fxe6 2 Qxe6+ Be7 3 Qc8+ Bd8 4 Qxb7 with 5 Qxa8. Black can try 4 ... Ne4, hoping for 5 Qxa8 Nxg3 6 hxg3 Qxh1 7 Qxb8 Bd3. But White still emerges on top with 5 Nxe4 Qxe4+ 6 Be3 (not 6 Be2 c5) 6 ... c5 7 Qxg7 Rf8 8 Bb5+ Nc6 9 Qb7 etc.

## 288.

1 Nd5 Bh4 (if 1 ... exd5 2 Qxe7 Rf7 3 Qd8+ Rf8 4 Qxd5+ winning a Rook) 2 Bxc7 Qa2 3 Nb4 winning Black's queen.

## 289.

1 Rxd7 Kxd7 2 Nc5+ Ke8 3 Bxc6+ Kf7 4 Qe6+ Kg6 5 Be4+ Kh6 6 Qh3#.

## 290.

1 Qg6 h6 2 Rxh6+ gxh6 3 Bxe5+ Rf6 4 Qxh6+ Qh7 5 Bxf6#.

## 291.

1 ... Bxh5 wins a pawn. If 2 Bxh5 the 2 ... Nxe4 threatening 3 ... Ng3+. The knight may not be taken: (a) 3 Qxe4 Rxh5+ 4 Qh4 Rxh4# (b) 3 dxe4 Qh3+ 4 Qh2 Qxh2+ 5 Kxh2 Rxh5#.

## 292.

1 Ne4 Qd8 2 Bxd5 cxd5 3 Qxd5 Qxd5 4 Nf6+ and 5 Nxd5 picks up a pawn.

## 293.

1 ... Qd3+ 2 Qe2 (otherwise ... Qxa6) 2 ... Rxe1+ 3 Kxe1 Bb4+ 4 Kf1 Qb1+ 5 Qe1 Qxe1#.

## 294.

1 ... Bh5 2 Ng4 Nf5 3 Qf2 Bxg4 4 hxg4 Rxg4+ 5 Kf1 Rg3 with 6 ... Rxe3, or 6 ... Rf3, or 6 ... Rxb3.

## 295.

Every knight move wins the queen, but the best is 1 Nxc6+. That's because you may not want to take the queen: 1 ... Kd7 (on 1 ... Kf7 you take 2 Qxh5+) 2 Re7+ Kc8 3 Nxa7+ Kb8 4 Qc7+ Kxa7 5 Qxb7#.

## 296.

1 Qxa6 bxa6 2 Rxb8+ Kxb8 3 Nc6+ Kc7 4 Nxe7 Bxe7 5 Bxh6.

## 297.

1 dxe5 Nxe5 2 Nxe5 Qxe5 3 Nd6 Rf8 (3 … Rd8 4 Nxf7) 4 Nxf7 Rxf7 5 Qd8+ Kh7 6 Bxf7.

## 298.

1 Bf6 Nxf6 2 Rxg7+ Kxg7 3 Rg1+ Kh8 4 Qe3 Nh7 5 Qh6 f5 6 Ng6+ Kg8 7 Nxf8+ Kh8 (if 7 … Kf7 8 Qxe6+ Kxf8 9 Rg8#) 8 Ng6+ Kg8 9 Ne7+ Kf7 10 Qxh7+ Ke8 11 Rg8+ Kd7 12 Bb5+.

## 299.

1 Rxc5 bxc5 2 Qd6+ Re7 3 Qe5 Re8 4 Qxc5+ Re7 5 Qe5 Rd7 (5 … Re8 6 Ba3+) 6 Qh8+ Ke7 7 Bf6+ Kd6 8 Qxa8.

## 300.

1 Qe3 is good enough but not 1 Rxe2? Rd1+ and mate next. Best is 1 Bf7+ Kd8 2 Qf8+ Kc7 3 Qe7+ Kc8 (3 … Kb6{b8} 4 Nd7+ wins the queen) 4 Be6+ Kb8 5 Nd7+ Kc7 (5 … Rxd7 6 Qe8+ Kc7 7 Qxd7+ and 8 Rxc2) 6 Nc5ı Kb6 7 Qxb7+ Kxc5 8 Qb4#.

## 300A.

Black's last move ( … Bc5) seems to create a nasty cross-pin, but it fails to 1 Qh7+ Kxh7 2 Rxg7+ Kh8 3 Rg8+ Kh7 4 R/1g7+ Kh6 5 Rg6+ Kh7 6 R/8g7+ Kh8 7 Rh6#.

## 300B.

1 … Rxg2 2 Rxg2 Rxg2 3 Kxg2 Qg6+ 4 Kh1 Bxe3 5 Nxe3 Nf2+ 6 Kh2 Nxd1 7 Nxd1 Bxf3.

# TACTICS INDEX

The numbers following each tactic represent the position numbers in this book.

Attraction: 116

Back rank: 148, 226, 249

Clearance: 9

Discovery : 14, 19, 38, 41, 45, 50, 65, 74, 85, 95, 101, 105, 112, 128, 136, 141, 243, 251, 254, 264, 270, 285, 295

Double attack (double threat): 21, 37, 92, 142, 163

Double check: 15

Driving off: 3, 18, 86, 92, 102, 118, 165, 167, 177, 184, 186, 210, 230, 233, 238, 247, 297

Draw: 162

En prise: 27, 56, 59, 66, 80, 90, 93, 94, 99, 168, 181, 185, 214, 216, 223, 245, 253, 272, 283

Fork: 34, 48, 55, 62, 64, 71, 88, 95, 97, 100A, 104, 119, 123, 125, 140, 147, 158, 166, 169, 171, 180, 183, 191, 193, 194, 196, 198, 203, 212, 217, 227, 250, 263, 281, 287, 292, 293

Get out of check: 246

Infiltration: 229

Interference: 39, 279

Line opening/closing: 108

Mating attack: 1, 5, 9, 12, 14, 17, 20, 25, 32, 33, 42, 43, 47, 49, 51, 57, 63, 68, 69, 100, 101, 110, 111, 114, 115, 116, 124, 127, 129, 131, 134, 137, 138, 139, 149, 150, 152, 154, 156, 161, 164, 175, 176, 179, 182, 187, 189, 190, 195, 199, 200A, 201, 207, 208, 211, 221, 224, 234, 235, 237, 240, 255, 256, 257, 258, 260, 261, 262, 267, 273, 275, 276, 277, 289, 290, 298, 300, 300A, 300B.

Overload: 8, 77, 133, 153, 160, 218, 248, 291

Pin: 4, 11, 12, 16, 23, 26, 29, 30, 35, 40, 44, 67, 75, 79, 82, 10 3, 113, 121, 130, 156, 172, 173, 200, 202, 205, 213, 239, 250, 269, 271, 294

Promotion: 22, 53, 91, 122, 192, 203, 204, 206, 225, 265, 282, 286

Removing the guard (deflection): 6, 13, 17, 24, 31, 33, 42, 43, 54, 58, 61, 63, 70, 72, 73, 78, 81, 89, 98, 105, 107, 109, 117, 125, 126, 127, 132, 135, 143, 145, 146, 151, 152, 174, 197, 209, 219, 220, 231, 236, 241, 242, 244, 268, 274, 278, 296, 299, 300A

Skewer: 60, 83, 104, 120, 222, 228, 232, 259, 280

Simplification (desperado): 52, 200B

Trapping: 2, 10, 28, 96, 100B, 106, 144, 155, 157, 170, 178, 188, 252, 284, 288

Unpin: 46, 76, 159, 266

X-ray: 87

Zwischenschach: 7, 84

Zugzwang: 215

# ABOUT THE AUTHORS

FRED WILSON is among the finest chess teachers and authors. He is the author of *A Picture History of Chess* and *101 Questions on How to Play Chess*. He edited *Classical Chess Matches: 1907–1913* and *Lesser-Known Chess Masterpieces: 1906–1915*. He is also the owner of Fred Wilson Chess Books in New York City and runs the web site www.fredwilsonchess.com.

BRUCE ALBERSTON is a well-known chess trainer and teacher in the New York City area and has recently written and narrated the best-selling CD-ROM, *Quick Kills on the Chessboard*. Alberston did significant research and analysis for Bruce Pandolfini (with whom he has written 17 chess books).

Wilson and Alberston have written four other books together: *303 Tactical Chess Puzzles*, *303 Tricky Checkmates*, *303 Tricky Chess Tactics*, and *202 Surprising Checkmates*.

# WHAT IS MENSA?

# Mensa
## The High IQ Society

Mensa is the international society for people with a high IQ. We have more than 100,000 members in over 40 countries worldwide.

The society's aims are:
- to identify and foster human intelligence for the benefit of humanity;
- to encourage research in the nature, characteristics, and uses of intelligence;
- to provide a stimulating intellectual and social environment for its members.

Anyone with an IQ score in the top two percent of the population is eligible to become a member of Mensa—are you the "one in 50" we've been looking for?

Mensa membership offers an excellent range of benefits:
- Networking and social activities nationally and around the world;
- Special Interest Groups (hundreds of chances to pursue your hobbies and interests—from art to zoology!);
- Monthly International Journal, national magazines, and regional newsletters;
- Local meetings—from game challenges to food and drink;
- National and international weekend gatherings and conferences;
- Intellectually stimulating lectures and seminars;

- Access to the worldwide SIGHT network for travelers and hosts.

For more information about Mensa International:
**www.mensa.org**
Mensa International
15 The Ivories
6–8 Northampton Street
Islington, London N1 2HY
United Kingdom

For more information about American Mensa:
**www.us.mensa.org**
Telephone: (817) 607-0060
American Mensa Ltd.
1229 Corporate Drive West
Arlington, TX 76006-6103 USA

For more information about British Mensa (UK and Ireland):
**www.mensa.org.uk**
Telephone: +44 (0) 1902 772771
E-mail: enquiries@mensa.org.uk
British Mensa Ltd.
St. John's House
St. John's Square
Wolverhampton WV2 4AH
United Kingdom